THE BRONX
It Was Only Yesterday, 1935-1965
1935-1965

THE
It Was

BRONX

Only Yesterday, 1935-1965

Lloyd Ultan / Gary Hermalyn

The Bronx County Historical Society
THE BRONX, NEW YORK

Designer: Henry C. Meyer, Jr.

THE BRONX IT WAS ONLY YESTERDAY, 1935-1965
is the third in a series of books by The Bronx County Historical
Society that documents the rich history and heritage, the social
life and customs of The Bronx and New York City. Unusual
and rare scenes from the Society's photograph and print collection
are featured in each of the books. Known as the *Life in The Bronx*
book series, the current available titles are:

THE BRONX IT WAS ONLY YESTERDAY, 1935-1965
by Lloyd Ultan & Gary Hermalyn

THE BEAUTIFUL BRONX, 1920-1950 by Lloyd Ultan

THE BRONX IN THE INNOCENT YEARS, 1890-1925
by Lloyd Ultan & Gary Hermalyn

ISBN 0-941980-33-2

CONTENTS

TO BRONXITES—
FOR NO MATTER WHERE THEY LIVE,
THE BRONX REMAINS A PART
OF THEIR LIVES

ACKNOWLEDGMENTS

We wish to thank the following people and organizations for their help in creating the photographic and vertical file collections of The Bronx County Historical Society.

Ms. Maralyn Alpert, Mr. Roger Arcara, Ms. Natalie Bassein, Mr. Frank Baxter, Mr. Ray Beckerman, Esq., Mr. Raymond Crapo, Mr. Joseph Duffy, Mr. Sol Elbaum, Mr. Robert Esnard, Mr. Robert Hall, Mr. and Mrs. Elias Karmon, Dr. Theodore Kazimiroff, Ms. Jacqueline Kutner, Mr. Sanford Lent, Mr. Max Levine, Mr. John McNamara, Mrs. Vivian J. Mall, Mr. Michael Miller, Mr. Tony Morante, Mr. Joseph Nardone, Ms. Bessie Wherry Noe, Mr. Ben Orange, Mr. Jimmy Packes, Ms. Rose Politi, Bro. Edward Quinn, Ms. Mary Russell, Rev. Abraham Salkowitz, Mr. Ron Schleissman, Mr. Ted Schleissman, Mr. Arthur Seifert, Mr. Anthony Signorelli and Louis and Sophie Ultan.

The Bronx Board of Trade, the Bronx Borough Engineer's Office, the Office of the President of the Borough of The Bronx, the Bronx Chamber of Commerce, the Bronx Oldtimers Association, the Bronx Press Review, Chester Studios, Cyrus Getter Associates, the Metropolitan Life Insurance Co., the New York City Department of Parks and Recreation, the New York City Department of Highways, the New York City Housing Authority, the New York Yankees and the Turner Construction Company.

We also want to express our gratitude to the fine staff of The Bronx County Historical Society: Ms. Ivette Arroyo, Education Aide; Ms. Madeline Cook, Library Clerk; Dr. Peter Derrick, Editor of *The Bronx County Historical Society Journal*; Ms. Lisa Garrison, Education Consultant; Ms. Katherine Gleeson, Senior Secretary; Ms. Mary Ilario, former photographic clerk; Ms. Kathleen A. McAuley, Curator; Ms. Kathleen Pacher, Secretary; Ms. Lisa Seifert, photographer; Ms. Myrna Sloam, former Librarian; Mrs. Laura Tosi, Associate Librarian; and Dr. Stephen Stertz, Researcher.

And finally, we thank the following people who assisted in the editing: Dr. Elizabeth Beirne, Mr. David Meth, Mr. Joel Podgor, and Mr. J.S. Weis.

THE BRONX
It Was Only Yesterday, 1935-1965
1935-1965

IT WAS ONLY YESTERDAY when we grew up in The Bronx. It is difficult to believe that the swirl of events changing our world between the middle of the Great Depression and the onset of the Great Society occurred such a short time ago. Yet, in the midst of this change, which had a great impact on each of us, The Bronx remained the center of our lives and the reference point from which we viewed and measured the life beyond the neighborhood in the rest of the world.

The New Deal's programs were on everyone's minds in the late 1930s

The New Deal's programs were on everyone's minds in the late 1930s. So many people we knew had the misfortune to be out of work and on, what was then called, home relief. For a father to have a job with the Works Progress Administration, or WPA, repairing the many streets or building new projects in The Bronx, was a stroke of good luck. With a steady income he could provide clothes and food for his family, and further, had the dignity of saying that he worked for what he got.

Indeed, in those few years before the onset of the Second World War, The Bronx seemed to be in a frenzy of construction, not all of it prompted by the federal government. The Bronx Terminal Market near Yankee Stadium was extended, improved, and opened with justifiable pride by Mayor Fiorello LaGuardia. Nearby, on the Grand Concourse, new, elegant, six-story apartment houses were built by private landlords in the fashionable Art Deco design, with cream-colored brick and casement windows. Those apartments were eagerly sought by the borough's up and coming people who knew that a Grand Concourse address was a badge of social status. In the Eastchester section of The Bronx, Governor Herbert Lehman opened the new Hillside Homes, whose ground level apartments became the most desirable for those who wanted access to the pretty gardens in the development.

More spectacular were the projects promoted by Robert Moses, the popular New York City Parks Commissioner and Chairman of the Triborough Bridge Authority. Under his leadership, St. Mary's Park in Mott Haven and Crotona Park, straddling the Tremont and Morrisania neighborhoods, were reconstructed. Moses was even able to get WPA money to build a giant new swimming pool and bathhouse in Crotona Park, and children from the surrounding neighborhoods flocked to the pool on sweltering summer days to dive into the cooling waters. In Pelham Bay Park, he also built a new public beach by pumping sand across the entrance to Pelham Bay itself, thus providing those of us living in The Bronx with our own nearby Orchard Beach along the gently lapping waters of Long Island Sound. Moses also erected the spectacular Triborough Bridge and the Major Deegan Expressway from it to the Grand Concourse. This unusual span, connecting three of the five boroughs, was opened by President Franklin Roosevelt himself, and enabled us in The Bronx to finally get to Queens without going by ferry or through Manhattan first. Bus service was provided from one end of the bridge to the other for those who did not have cars. Similarly, Moses also built the Henry Hudson Bridge, a huge steel arch spanning the Harlem River Ship Canal which led motorists from midtown Manhattan beside the banks of the Hudson River onto the new Henry Hudson Parkway built through the Spuyten Duyvil and Riverdale sections of The Bronx and then through Van Cortlandt Park to connect with the Saw Mill River Parkway in Westchester County.

The building frenzy seemed as if it would never stop. The federal government opened a new Bronx Central Post Office, on the Grand Concourse and 149th Street, even though The Bronx was still administratively linked to Manhattan's Post Office, and we were still to sign the return address on our letters, not The Bronx, but "New York, N.Y." The murals inside the lobby depicting all sorts of work done by city and country laborers throughout the nation were done by Ben Shahn and his wife who had won a special national competition to get the job. The federal government also financed the construction of the nearby Bronx County Jail on Gerard Avenue. Robert Moses, only a few years after completing the Triborough Bridge, built the Bronx-Whitestone Bridge to replace the Clason Point ferry service that had connected the eastern part of The Bronx to Queens. He also completed the conversion of the old Williamsbridge Reservoir near Bainbridge Avenue and 208th Street into Reservoir Oval Park, thus providing the people of that neighborhood with a large playground and sports facility. Perhaps, the biggest private construction project undertaken at the time was done by the Metropolitan Life Insurance Company. The giant firm took over the grounds of the venerable Catholic Protectory between the Morris Park and Unionport neighborhoods to build a red-brick private housing complex complete with landscaped grounds, play areas, and shopping which they called Parkchester. It was the company's experiment in planned affordable housing, and it proved to be a great success, as well as the largest housing development in the country at its completion.

Even the great seats of higher learning were expanding in those waning days of the Great Depression. Fordham University erected its Gothic-towered Keating Hall on its campus where it overlooked Southern Boulevard and the New York Botanical Garden beyond. Similarly, at the tip of Throggs Neck, the old Fort Schuyler was converted for use as the New York State Maritime Academy to teach marine engineering and to prepare its cadets for service in the nation's merchant marine. The new institution joined not only Fordham University, but the Bronx campus of New York University, Manhattan College, the College of Mount Saint Vincent and Hunter College in The Bronx. It is no wonder that Bronx Borough President James J. Lyons proudly proclaimed The Bronx as "The Borough of Universities."

The bombing of Pearl Harbor, however, swept the country into World War II, and we Bronx residents rose to the challenge. Some young men enlisted in the cause, others were drafted, and we at the home front contributed what we could to the war effort. We dutifully bought war bonds, gathered old pots and pans for scrap metal drives, hung little white banners in our windows bearing a blue star for each family serviceman, observed meatless Tuesdays, handed over the required number of ration stamps to buy such scarce items as sugar, and drew down the black window shades at night so that no light could escape into the street to alert possible enemy bombers. There were, of course, more women than men in the streets each day, and many of them had jobs for the first time because most working men were in the armed forces. Starlight Amusement Park along the Bronx River in West Farms was closed and its massive Coliseum was taken over by the army for a truck depot. The Memorial Day parade up the Grand Concourse allowed for an outpouring of patriotism as bands and veterans in the American Legion and other organizations were joined by young men in khaki not yet assigned to the front.

Oddly, most ordinary life remained relatively untouched. At the beginning, even though the amount of new construction was necessarily diminished, it did not end. The Catholic Archdiocese managed to open the new Cardinal Hayes High School on the Grand Concourse and 152nd Street, Lebanon Hospital rose further up the Concourse on Mount Eden Avenue, and the Metropolitan Life Insurance Company managed to complete its huge Parkchester development.

. . . proclaimed The Bronx as "The Borough of Universities"

Most people used public transportation to get to Manhattan and to travel within The Bronx

Most people used public transportation to get to Manhattan and to travel within The Bronx, and were thus unaffected by the government's gas rationing measures. They still paid their nickel to travel by subway or elevated train, trolley, or bus. In fact, it was fun. Most of the subway lines were elevated in The Bronx, and a panorama of neighborhoods passed by as the train wended its way down the track toward Manhattan. The Third Avenue El, of course, continued providing its views even after it crossed the Harlem River, but when the Woodlawn-Jerome line plunged into a tunnel just south of Yankee Stadium, or the White Plains Road line did so just before the Third Avenue station at 149th Street, or the Pelham Bay line did so before the Hunts Point Avenue station, all such views were cut off. The newly-built IND line under the Grand Concourse, and the newly-acquired Dyre Avenue line, which was operated as a shuttle to the White Plains Road line's 180th Street station, unfortunately were not elevated, and provided no such views. Trolleys, painted yellow with red trim, rode along tracks imbedded in the street and were powered by an electric line suspended overhead. They provided a smooth ride through most Bronx neighborhoods. In the summertime, the wooden sides were taken off the cars and they were replaced by iron mesh to allow for cool breezes as the trolley moved through the streets. Buses were less used, and appeared largely on the Grand Concourse, 170th Street, and Pelham Parkway although there were other bus routes. Unlike the trolleys, however, the buses could not remove their sides in the summer, and a ride at that time on a bus could be blisteringly hot.

People still sought their primary entertainment in neighborhood movie houses, usually belonging to the Loew's or RKO chains. Every neighborhood had its own movie theater, such as the Ogden in Highbridge, the Park Plaza in Morris Heights, or the Interboro in Throggs Neck, and a tired and war-weary public sought escape and inspiration from the double feature presentations they saw there on the silver screen. Some theaters, however, were special, none more so than the Loew's Paradise, on the Grand Concourse and 188th Street. Here was a world apart, a fantasy land come true. The attraction of the Paradise was not just its double presentations, but the opulence of its architecture and its decorations. A lobby filled with sculpture and baroque-style paintings, a Seth Thomas clock, and a fountain filled with huge gold fish immediately swept the patron out of his ordinary world. The immense 4,000-seat theatre boasted of walls filled with copies of Renaissance sculpture and imitation cypress trees to impart the effect of an Italian garden, all covered by a dark blue ceiling with twinkling lights to simulate stars, and real clouds floating across the night sky to complete the illusion. The Paradise was for a special Saturday night date, or an evening out with the family, especially since this theater showed films directly after their downtown run. Crowds gathered outside the theater for every evening performance, dressed in their best clothes, and kept in order by uniformed ushers.

At home, people listened to radio with its variety of music, news, drama, and comedy. For anyone with relatives in Europe or a son in the army, the radio immediately brought news of great importance to the family into the living room. Indeed, it was one of the main ties that bound The Bronx to the rest of the nation and the wider world. Like the movies, however, the radio was also used as a means to escape from everyday cares and the worries of the war. Programs, such as *Fred Allen, Jack Benny,* and *The Great Gildersleeve,* all provided needed laughter. *The Make Believe Ballroom* and *Your Hit Parade* filled the house with the popular music of the day to rid the mind of its usual cares, and drama shows, such as *Suspense, Lux Radio Theater,* and *The FBI in Peace and War,* would fire the imagination by painting scenes in words. One of the most popular drama shows was *The Goldbergs,* written and starring Gertrude Berg as a Bronx housewife presiding over her Jewish family living on Tremont Avenue while facing and solving problems with good sense and gentle humor. Their problems were similar to those we faced every day.

Despite the war, school children continued to attend the neighborhood public or parochial schools where the standard of education was very high. The main difference between the two groups seemed to be that the parochial schools demanded their pupils wear some sort of school uniform, while the public schools required merely that boys wear white shirts and a red tie, and that girls be attired in neat dresses. Of course, religious instruction was given in the parochial schools, but even in the public ones, weekly assemblies were opened with a Bible reading and the singing of a hymn, as well as the recitation of the Pledge of Allegiance and the singing of the national anthem. No one seemed to mind. Indeed, after the school day was over and during the long summer, the many parks and playgrounds in The Bronx still echoed with the laughter of children from all the schools playing together.

Even during the war, with all of its shortages of food and other goods, the neighborhood groceries, restaurants, cafeterias, and specialty shops still catered to the immediate family needs. Each neighborhood in The Bronx had its own character. Although many ethnic groups could live in a single neighborhood, each area was usually dominated by one group. Prosperous Irish preferred living in private or row houses, while those with less of an income found accommodations in apartments. Thus, the Irish dominated Mott Haven, with its frame houses interspersed with turn-of-the-century apartments and older row houses. They were also the major ethnic group in Highbridge, in Kingsbridge, and in Parkchester, the huge red brick housing development built by the Metropolitan Life Insurance Company. Many Jews dwelled in apartment houses built both before and after the First World War in Hunts Point and in Morrisania. Affluent Jews resided along the tree-lined Grand Concourse, or on the adjoining side streets, which were flanked by new, elegant Art Deco style apartment houses attended by uniformed doormen. Italians lived predominantly in Melrose and Belmont, neighborhoods with a mixture of private houses and small apartment buildings. They also favored the suburban and rural atmosphere of the northeastern quadrant of the borough. Blacks lived near the Melrose station of the New York Central Railroad, and in the private houses in Wakefield. The wealthiest families in The Bronx, such as the Dodges and Delafields, lived in mansions on estates in Riverdale, while people with a nautical bent favored the nineteenth century frame houses set amid the seafood restaurants and marinas of City Island. Others of a similar view preferred areas along Long Island Sound in Throggs Neck and Clason Point. Interspersed among these and the Bronx neighborhoods could also be found appreciable numbers of Germans, Scandinavians, Puerto Ricans, Armenians, Chinese, and other groups.

Somehow, despite some cultural differences, we generally got along. The people who lived in the neighborhood, no matter what their income, all believed in the middle class values of working hard to earn a wage or salary, of paying in full for whatever was purchased, of enjoying a warm, close family life, and of trying to make life better for the children, especially through education. For most people, religious traditions were also important. They not only attended their neighborhood church

Each neighborhood in The Bronx had its own character

or synagogue to partake in prayer, but faithfully observed religious holidays and holy days, and attended family confirmations, bar mitzvahs, and weddings. The neighborhood church or synagogue was also a center of social life, with its picnics, organized outings, dances, bazaars, and shows. In almost every neighborhood, the local teacher, policeman, fireman, mailman, or clergyman was likely to live nearby, and even to reside next door.

The pressures of war, however, promoted change in The Bronx. The building of new houses came to a halt during the conflict, but more people flocked to New York City to take advantage of new job openings. In addition, the Harlem and East Harlem neighborhoods in northern Manhattan were dangerously overcrowded. Starting in 1943, increasing numbers of Blacks and Puerto Ricans moved out of those areas to live in the large apartments located near transportation, shopping, and parks available in Hunts Point and Morrisania. As with the other ethnic groups which preceded them, they came because The Bronx was better. Their children joined those who were already in the classroom, and the parents were elected to office in the local Parent-Teachers Associations. Those of us growing up at the time regularly included the new neighbors in such street games as stickball, stoopball, potsie, jacks, and skipping rope.

The housing crunch came after the war ended in 1945. Following several days of anxious waiting for the announcement of Japan's surrender to be officially proclaimed over the radio that August, a disembodied voice finally stated that the conflict had ceased. General jubilation ensued. Neighbors hugged and kissed each other. Some leaned out of apartment windows to yell joyous shouts of victory in relief and gratitude that the great ordeal was over. Others danced in the streets. In the months that followed, men in uniform were discharged and came back to their families and their neighborhoods. After a party given to celebrate each one's safe arrival, the former serviceman picked up the threads of his life.

Desiring to quickly make up for missed years of normal living, recently discharged men soon married girlfriends and tried to find places to reside. The housing shortage made this difficult to do. As a temporary remedy, two instant neighborhoods of quonset huts were built on large empty lots in Soundview and Castle Hill. The quonset hut, a small, tubular device of corrugated metal having two of its sides curving upward to become part of a semi-circular arched roof, provided the minimum space needed until more permanent housing could be found. Concrete walkways afforded paths between the huts. A few enterprising newly-married women planted some flowers in the strips of dirt between their own metal structure and the concrete path.

The city government took the lead in providing permanent housing. In many neighborhoods, blocks of old frame and brick houses were torn down to construct tall red brick apartment house projects with modest rents. While the rooms were small, the facilities were new, and the buildings were set amid large swaths of grass and trees dotted with small playgrounds.

People who had gone through the hardships of the Great Depression were not only willing, but eager, to agree with government that it should provide adequate shelter for the less well off. Thus, from the late 1940s, through the 1950s, and into the 1960s, clusters of projects rose high over neighboring five-and six-story apartment houses which were previously the tallest residential structures in most areas. Whether it was the John Purroy Mitchell Houses in Mott Haven, the Highbridge

Houses in Highbridge, the Forest Neighborhood Houses and the Claremont Neighborhood Houses in Morrisania, the Castle Hill Houses in Castle Hill, the Sedgwick Houses in Morris Heights, the Pelham Parkway Houses on Pelham Parkway, or others scattered throughout the borough, the projects eased the housing shortage and provided decent dwellings for those who needed them at a low rent.

Private developers soon followed suit, building single family attached, semi-detached, and unattached houses on previously empty lots in Throggs Neck, Eastchester, Soundview, and other neighborhoods in the eastern and northern reaches of The Bronx. Later they also erected tall "luxury" apartment houses, often with terraces, such as Concourse Village south of 161st Street and Morris Avenue, and the Executive Towers on the Grand Concourse at 165th Street. Many such apartment houses were built in the Spuyten Duyvil and Riverdale neighborhoods. With technological developments, the newest houses were provided with sleeves through the brick walls beneath windows in which the occupant could place air conditioners. This amenity replaced the awnings, which, in the older buildings, were used to shade the window from the sun. Indeed, by the 1960s, many residents of the older apartments purchased air conditioners and mounted them on window sills, so they, too, could enjoy their cooling effect during a sweltering summer.

Of course, all of this new construction helped ease the housing crisis. Many former servicemen and an appreciable number of those who lived in older houses in Hunts Point, Morrisania, and Mott Haven moved into the new privately-built housing in other parts of The Bronx or in the growing suburbs, while others moved into the brand new projects. The vacated apartments and houses in these neighborhoods then became available to more Blacks and Puerto Ricans coming up from Manhattan. Thus, by the end of the 1950s, Blacks dominated Morrisania, while Puerto Ricans were concentrated in Hunts Point and Mott Haven.

The servicemen returning from the war not only affected housing, they also affected schools. Spurred by the federal law popularly known as the GI Bill, which provided government funds for their tuition, many jumped at the chance to obtain what they otherwise could not afford: a college education. For the first time, large numbers of older men who had left high school years earlier could be found on such Bronx campuses as Fordham, New York University, Manhattan College, and C.C.N.Y. in Manhattan, eagerly taking notes in classes and doing research in libraries and laboratories in a serious and feverish attempt to learn all they could to get a good job after graduation and to earn more than their fathers did.

On no campus did the ex-servicemen have a greater effect than on Hunter College in The Bronx. After serving as a temporary first home to the United Nations Security Council, the campus was returned to the college's administration, and it was opened to men as well as women. This was the first time that the renowned women's institution admitted men into its classes, although it was not until 1955 that a freshman class there had an equal number of both sexes.

Before the end of the 1950s, the increasing demand for college facilities led to two new institutions of higher education finding a home in what was widely-known as the Borough of Universities. Yeshiva University began building its Albert Einstein College of Medicine in the Morris Park neighborhood, and the new Bronx Community College began admitting students on Field Place west of the Grand Concourse in an old structure once used by the Bronx High School of Science and designed to look like a French chateau.

Of longer lasting effect on the borough's schools was the desire of the former servicemen and their new brides to start families as soon as possible. Maternity wards of Fordham Hospital near Southern Boulevard, or Dr. Leff's at Morris Avenue and the Grand Concourse, or Parkchester General Hospital, or any of the many other hospitals in The Bronx were overtaxed as available beds for childbirth were at a premium. As the newborns grew in the security of their homes and neighborhoods, they eventually reached school age. When they did, classrooms became overcrowded and facilities were stretched to the breaking point. The public high school system of Morris, Evander Childs, Roosevelt, Clinton, Bronx High School of Science, Jane Addams, Columbus, Gompers, Dodge Vocational, Monroe, Taft and Walton had very high attendance figures and extra sessions. New schools were erected, additions were made to some existing schools, and some buildings with obsolete facilities were destroyed to be replaced by new ones on the site. The Catholic Archdiocese was especially active, opening several new parochial high schools, mostly in the northern and eastern sections of The Bronx where new housing had attracted more and growing families. Preston, Monsignor Scanlon, and St. Helena High Schools were established in Throggs Neck, Cardinal Spellman High School was built in Eastchester, and St. Raymond High School bordered on Parkchester.

As the children grew, they affected the use of parks, playgrounds, and streets. For several years after the end of the war, mothers could be seen walking the streets and sitting on the wooden benches in the tree-shaded parks tending their youngsters in their baby carriages. As they grew, the toddlers rambled over the hills and rocks and ran through the shrubbery and green fields of the parks. Eventually, they became big enough to ride the swings, whoosh down the slides, and balance each other on the see-saws in the many playgrounds of The Bronx.

When the boys were old enough, they began to play games in the streets which they learned from still older boys. Variations of baseball which had been played by their parents as children were still popular. They were all played with a pink rubber ball manufactured by the Spaulding Company, which everyone called a "spauldeen." This ball was used by a boy to bounce against the point of a step of a building to play stoopball, or off the point of the sidewalk curb to play curbball, or to hit with a fist to play punchball, or to hit with a broomhandle to play stickball. The "spauldeen" was versatile enough to also be used in playing handball or paddleball off apartment house, schoolyard, or playground walls; king-queen (a juvenile version of handball), which needed a wall and the sidewalk squares; and boxball, in which only the sidewalk squares were used. The streets were also used for pitching pennies, flipping baseball trading cards, playing potzie, playing marbles, and a variety of other games. Sometimes, the space between the lowest and next to lowest rung of a ladder hanging vertically from an apartment house fire escape was pressed into service for use as a hoop to play a game of basketball. As more playgrounds were built with basketball courts laid out on their asphalt grounds, boys could play the real game.

As the 1950s progressed, sports for boys became more organized. Uniformed baseball teams were established, and whole Little Leagues instituted. In the spring, boys from the teams of the Highbridge, Castle Hill, Mosholu, and other Little Leagues would get dressed in their uniforms, wear their cleated shoes, and, carrying

. . . a pink rubber ball manufactured by the Spaulding Company

their bats and gloves, march in formation to the nearest field established in the neighborhood to play their games. Adult volunteers acted as managers and coaches, and proud parents cheered as their offspring made a key hit or a spectacular fielding play, or just enjoyed the game.

The fact that parents could afford to spend the funds needed to buy basketballs or baseball equipment testified to the expanding prosperity of The Bronx following the war. The jobs obtained by the returning serviceman often proved higher paying, especially for a person who had weathered the ordeal of the Great Depression and the deprivation of the home front of World War II. Moreover, the number of jobs expanded so rapidly that it was not unusual for one man to be able to hold down two of them. For those who were used to working long hours for little money in the past, the extra time put in for so much more take-home pay was not that much of a hardship. Even those who held only one job could now afford to buy material goods they had wished for, in part because of lower prices caused by the availability of increasing numbers of products following the country's conversion to a peacetime economy. This included the installation of a telephone, and, within a few years after the war, almost every family had one in their home.

Bronx families were helped because prices remained fairly steady throughout the 1950s and early 1960s. The short burst of inflation which had hit the country following the end of the war had abated to a rate of about one percent a year. Moreover, customers discovered the utility of the installment plan. In stores along such major shopping streets as Third Avenue, Tremont Avenue, and Webster Avenue near Fordham Road, for a small down payment, a family could buy furniture or other expensive items without first saving large sums, and the rest of the cost of the purchase would be paid off with a small amount each month that included part of the principle and an interest payment set at a low rate.

The growing prosperity thus contributed to the change of life in The Bronx. Television was thought a science fiction novelty before the war. In fact, when one was displayed in the lounge of the Earl Theater on 161st Street near River Avenue in the late 1930s, the set was so bulky and the screen so tiny compared to the movie theater screen that the consensus was that no one would ever buy one. Nevertheless, when Milton Berle first appeared on television in the *Texaco Star Theatre* in 1948, a demand arose to see the famous comedian. One after another, into the early 1950s, people began to purchase television sets, large wooden console models with sixteen-inch screens, often bearing wooden doors to close off the blackened screen when not in use. Tuesday nights at eight o'clock, when Milton Berle cavorted in his comedy skits and introduced a variety of vaudeville acts, the streets of The Bronx were deserted. Those who had not bought television sets yet were invited into neighbor's homes to see the new electronic marvel and to enjoy the entertainment, seated in a blackened room as if they were in a movie theater. They soon began saving to purchase their own sets, and within five years, it seemed as if almost a majority of families in The Bronx had one. So wondrous was this new medium that when stores selling television sets opened at the Hub or Fordham Road and displayed their wares in their windows, people stopped walking along the sidewalks and gathered in front of the display windows to watch the show being aired on the new marvel.

Even more than radio, television bound us in The Bronx to the wider world. Night after night, a whole new world of entertainment flickered into the living

Television was thought a science fiction novelty before the war

rooms of The Bronx, and we knew that people all over the country were watching the same thing at the same time. On the television set were seen the black and white images of Sid Caesar and Imogene Coca in *Your Show of Shows,* which featured Carl Reiner from the Tremont neighborhood of The Bronx, and Ed Sullivan in *The Toast of the Town.* Shows already familiar to those who had listened to radio, such as *The Adventures of Ozzie and Harriet, Gunsmoke,* and The Bronx's own *The Goldbergs,* also made the transition to the new medium. Other shows, such as *The Kraft Television Theatre* and *Philco Playhouse,* specialized in plays written especially for television. It was for these that Paddy Chayefsky from The Bronx wrote *Marty* and *The Catered Affair,* two original television plays set in the borough. *I Love Lucy,* starring Lucille Ball and Desi Arnaz, pioneered the half hour situation comedy, and was also the first television show to be filmed instead of being telecast live. Saturday mornings were reserved for children's cartoon shows, such as old *Out of the Inkwell* and *Betty Boop* productions from the early days of sound films. There was also a large dose of Hollywood westerns, especially Hopalong Cassidy films, fed to the youngsters, who, in earlier days, would have been playing cowboys and Indians in St. Mary's, Claremont, or another neighborhood park. They also watched *Howdy Doody* every afternoon, and *Disneyland* on Sunday nights. Sunday afternoons were set aside for intellectual and public information shows, such as *Meet the Press, Omnibus,* and *You Are There,* the program which brought its audience back in time by having modern news reporters interview actors playing historical characters in a historical event.

As time passed, Ed Wynn, Jack Benny, Eddie Cantor, Jackie Gleason, Red Skelton, and other comedians obtained their own variety shows. Later, Dinah Shore, Perry Como, Kate Smith, and other popular singers replaced the comedians as the hosts of such television offerings. Variety shows also extended into the late night realm, with Jerry Lester in *Broadway Open House* pioneering, to be followed by *The Tonight Show* starring Steve Allen, featuring the young singer, Eydie Gorme, from The Bronx. It seemed that every day, conversation between Bronx residents had to include each person's opinions of the previous evening's shows, and reactions and reviews thus obtained were eagerly exchanged.

Television also brought the world indoors. The set changed the arrangement of furniture in almost every living room in The Bronx, as chairs and sofas were positioned to face the large box with its flickering screen. No one dared talk as people watched with rapt attention to the gavel to gavel coverage of the Democratic and Republican National Conventions, the pomp and ceremony of the inauguration of Presidents Eisenhower and Kennedy, the Army-McCarthy Hearings, the Kefauver Crime Committee Hearings, sessions of the United Nations Security Council on the crisis in the Middle East and in the Congo, the assassination of President Kennedy and the shooting of Lee Harvey Oswald. News programs, such as the *Camel News Caravan* and *Douglas Edwards with the News,* brought images of the events of the day into every living room in The Bronx. The world became a much smaller place.

With entertainment moving indoors, much of the life of the Bronx streets was affected. Stores began closing earlier. Families who once enjoyed itinerant street singers roaming from neighborhood to neighborhood and into backyards of apartment houses now found a much greater variety on television. In addition, the opportunity for steady jobs increased so that no one was forced to subsist on show-

With entertainment moving indoors, much of the life of the Bronx streets was affected

ers of coins raining down upon him from many Bronx apartment windows as in the past in appreciation of his singing. Consequently, the number of street singers in The Bronx declined, and, by the middle of the 1950s, disappeared. Similarly, the itinerant street peddler sharpening knives and scissors or purchasing used clothing, yelling "I cash clothes," also passed from the scene. The ice man who brought a cake of ice from his truck by carrying it by huge tongs as it rested on a cloth draped over his stooped back to the ice box in the kitchen also disappeared as ice boxes were replaced by gas and electric refrigerators. Certainly, the loss of these people left the streets less colorful than they were in the past.

Radio entertainment was also affected by the increasing popularity of television. Now that drama and variety could be seen as well as heard, both declined on radio. *The Big Show,* which featured some of the biggest names in music and comedy each Sunday night, was the last attempt to mount a major new radio variety program, while some other shows, such as *Arthur Godfrey's Talent Scouts,* appeared on television while simulcasting the sound over radio as well. Soon, even these programs abandoned the older medium. From that point, each radio station began to specialize in broadcasting recorded music, news, and sports events.

The new era, which brought television sets into almost every living room in The Bronx, also had an affect upon movies, which had previously been the major form of public entertainment. Hollywood first retaliated with spectacular productions, often three hours long, which no television show could possibly match. Partially because of this, the old double feature began to disappear, initially in the first-run theaters in Manhattan. The admission price was now good only for one motion picture, not two. Of course, when the film was a color spectacle, such as *Samson and Delilah, The Greatest Show on Earth, Ben Hur, The Three Musketeers* or *The Ten Commandments,* no one seemed to mind. These spectacles, usually as long as two normal motion pictures, also played without a second movie when shown in The Bronx. Otherwise, the double feature continued as usual at the neighborhood movie house.

Hollywood also touted new photographic processes. Cinerama, a three-camera projection system, could only be used in a specially equipped theatre, and was installed in the Warner's in Manhattan. Thus, it was never shown in The Bronx. Many a Bronxite, however, would take the subway to Times Square just to experience the novelty. Another experiment was 3-D. Here, cardboard-framed green polaroid plastic lenses were distributed to paying patrons in order for them to see the process properly. The film could have been *Bwana Devil* or *The House of Wax.* Nevertheless, the cardboard-framed lenses proved to be uncomfortable, and viewing through them often hurt the eyes and gave the wearer a headache. A more successful process was CinemaScope, which was first used in the film, *The Robe.* Here, the camera produced a wider picture and most theatres in The Bronx quickly installed wider screens to accommodate the new process.

The motion picture producers also attempted to attract patrons with new stars. Certainly, the most celebrated was the voluptuous Marilyn Monroe. Some Bronx teenagers, contemplating a Saturday night date at the Loew's Paradise, sang a ditty to the tune of "Stranger in Paradise," from a current Broadway show, *Kismet*:

. . . the itinerant street peddler . . . yelling "I cash clothes"

Take my toe,
I'm a stranger in the Paradise,
All lost in the second row,
While watching Marilyn Monroe.

The more demure Doris Day attracted other Bronx fans, especially in her sophisticated comedies with Rock Hudson. Grace Kelly was a classic beauty. Dean Martin and Jerry Lewis formed the most popular comedy team of the time. Marlon Brando showed acting brilliance in his pictures, while brooding James Dean appealed to the younger crowd. Gene Kelly was noted for his athletic dancing style. All of them were topics for discussion among Bronx moviegoers, some of whom grew up with two of the new stars who came from The Bronx. Sal Mineo burst on the scene at the same time as James Dean, and Tony Curtis, really Bernie Schwartz from Hunts Point, caused unexpected hilarity with his Bronx accent when he starred in *The Black Shield of Falworth,* set in the Middle Ages.

Although the movies were a popular place to go in the 1950s, Bronxites did not go as often as in the past. The movie theater, however, was still a favorite destination for a Saturday night date, and the Loew's Paradise and the RKO Fordham near the intersections of Fordham Road and the Grand Concourse remained popular. On the other hand, the new Hollywood processes were not enough to save the smaller theatres which had specialized in showing third-run movies. The Fleetwood Theater, for example, on Morris Avenue just south of 165th Street became a bowling alley, and the Zenith Theatre on 170th Street just west of Jerome Avenue closed its doors forever.

The movie houses had also to compete with other forms of amusement as well. Bowling became a big attraction. In almost every neighborhood, bowling alleys opened. They were touted as clean, wholesome, family fun. The owners also offered a selection of bowling balls for those who did not own one, and they rented bowling shoes as well. Not only families, but many teenagers on dates would spend one evening a week at such bowling alleys as Stadium Bowling across the street from Yankee Stadium and Paradise Lanes across the Grand Concourse from the Loew's Paradise Theatre. Many men and women enrolled in bowling leagues which engaged in tournaments, and the winning teams would receive trophies. At first, pinboys located beyond the end of the alley were responsible for clearing the downed pins and setting up new ones for the next bowler. When machines were invented to do that job, however, almost every alley installed them, and the games seemed to proceed at a faster pace. Some Bronx customers, however, seemed to enjoy the slower, more deliberate methods of the pinboys who continued to be employed at the Decatur Lanes.

Even those who went bowling once a week, had the opportunity to use other recreational facilities in The Bronx for their enjoyment. Some Bronxites preferred the atmosphere of the pool halls, several of which also featured bowling, as did the establishment in the basement at 167th Street between Walton and Gerard Avenues across the street from the rear of Morrisania Hospital. Others went skating at the rink on Jerome Avenue south of Fordham Road. Those who wanted to go swimming, had their choice of several pools, including the Bronxdale Pool, the Bronx Beach and Pool, and the Jerome Beach and Pool Club, formerly Cascades. Golfers could choose courses in Van Cortlandt and Pelham Bay Parks, and miniature golf courses seemed to sprout up on almost every remaining empty lot in each neighbor-

Bowling became a big attraction

11

hood. Those who wanted to go horseback riding had the use of bridle paths in Van Cortlandt Park near Broadway, along Pelham Parkway, and in Pelham Bay Park. Boats for rowing were available at the lakes in Crotona Park and in Van Cortlandt Park, while those who owned boats docked them at marinas on Long Island Sound at City Island, Throggs Neck, and Clason Point. By the early 1960s, even a ski slope was made available in winter on the hills of one of the Van Cortlandt Park golf courses.

Reading books remained popular in the 1950s. This was aided by the extensive New York Public Library system in The Bronx. Schools encouraged children to use the libraries and to borrow books on a regular basis. It was not uncommon to see both children and adults trek to the nearest branch, whether it was the Morrisania, Woodstock, Fordham, Kingsbridge, or other neighborhood branches of the New York Public Library to return books, browse the shelves for ones they had not read, and to borrow those which had caught their fancy. The choice of books was no longer confined to the libraries. Some stores opened lending libraries and rented new hardcover best sellers to their patrons, and local candy stores in almost every Bronx neighborhood began to stock paperback books in increasing number to sell to their customers. For about a quarter, a person could buy a popular novel without worrying about returning it. Such a book could be savored and treasured. It was not uncommon to see Bronx teenagers clutching a paperback copy of *A Stone for Danny Fisher* or *A Catcher in the Rye* while walking in the street.

Newspapers were also affected by the new prosperity. Because of the explosion of entertainment and communication provided by television, newspapers no longer served as the primary source of information. The expanding focus upon world events begun during the war and expressed in part by television caused the old Bronx *Home News* to cease publication in 1948. For decades, this afternoon newspaper had provided information about happenings and functions in the local neighborhood, and it had been distributed door to door by a small army of schoolboys trying to earn money after school hours. Its assets were purchased by the *New York Post* which initially provided some Bronx news on a daily basis, but, by 1955, decreased it to two columns appearing in a special Bronx edition. The only newspaper to try to cover the news of the entire borough was the *Bronx Press-Review*, a weekly, which had begun as the house newspaper for Parkchester and which had expanded to fill the void. In any case, the *Home News* was an institution sorely missed by its faithful readers.

Even, as the borough's own daily newspaper declined into oblivion, there was more news to cover in The Bronx. Edward J. Flynn, the county's Democratic Party boss, who had backed Franklin Roosevelt and Harry Truman for the presidency, suddenly died in 1952, and was replaced by Congressman Charles Buckley. Flynn, who had explained his political methods in his autobiography, *You're the Boss*, was able to control events. He was powerful enough to induce both Roosevelt and Truman to campaign for votes in The Bronx while they occupied the White House, and thousands lined the motorcade routes to cheer them when they passed.

While Buckley was as tough as Flynn, he was buffeted by the forces of change in The Bronx. His leadership of the party was challenged by a younger group of Democrats, mostly Jews, Blacks, and Puerto Ricans who felt left out of the decision-making process. They called themselves Reformers, and their effort to gain control of the party structure weakened the almost total control by the Democrats of Bronx political life. For instance, Republican Paul Fino was able to capture the congressional seat from the northeast Bronx, and Republican Joseph F. Periconi actually won the race for Bronx Borough President in 1960 when James J. Lyons, who had been a fixture in that post, retired. Yet, Buckley remained powerful enough to get John F. Kennedy, the 1960 presidential candidate, to campaign in The Bronx at a huge rally on the Grand Concourse south of Fordham Road. There, the candidate revealed that he was a Bronxite because he had lived years earlier in Riverdale. After the rally, he motorcaded down the Grand Concourse for a dinner at the Concourse Plaza Hotel on 161st Street.

Those who had reached their teenage years in The Bronx during this period sought to place their own imprint on their world. This extended into the realm of music. The lilting rhythms of jazz and popular ballads which dominated the early 1950s soon gave way to the driving beat of such early Rock n' Roll hits as "Rock Around the Clock." While Elvis Presley and his gyrating pelvis drove teenagers into spasms of ecstasy, parents generally disapproved. They preferred the new Latin beat of the Cha Cha or the Mambo. The new Rock n' Roll beat, nevertheless, was championed by younger disc jockeys on radio, and by Dick Clark, whose television show, called *American Bandstand,* made the entire new generation aware of the latest trends. At times, a Bronx high school, such as Taft or St. Nicholas of Tolentine, would be invited to send representatives to dance on the show. The slow dancing which was appropriate for the old popular ballads was replaced by the more energetic Savoy, Lindy, Bunny Hop, Twist, and other dances which tended to separate the two dancing partners and emphasize their individual gyrating bodies.

Almost every teenage boy and girl knew the latest hits on the new 45 rpm records. The records had a wide hole in the center which could be played only on a phonograph specially made or adapted for their use. With a stack of records and a 45 rpm player with an automatic record changer to eliminate frequent manual changing of records once one was finished, anyone could hold a party in their house or apartment in The Bronx.

Some were encouraged by the popularity of the new music to band together in small groups from the neighborhood to sing the new hits or new songs written by one of their members, usually *a cappella* in hallways, in basements, or in alleys to get a nice sound. Some of the groups formed proved to have good voices and a musical sense to tempt them to turn professional once their members graduated from high school. That is what happened to Dion and the Belmonts, who took their name from their own Bronx neighborhood. One Bronxite who became a singing star on his own was Bobby Darin, who launched his career after graduating from Bronx High School of Science.

Teenagers also made their own statement in fashions. By the mid-1950s, new colors, such as shocking pink and chartreuse, became popular, especially for jackets which indicated that the wearers were all members of the same teenage club. Some girls preferred wearing tight toreador pants and combing their hair into a ponytail. Some boys sported chino pants, rolled their short sleeves on their white T-shirts up to the shoulder joint, or raised the collar of their dress shirts to cover the nape of their necks, and wore their hair in pompadours in front with the sides slicked back to form a duck's tail in the rear. In cooler weather, there were some who preferred to wear black leather jackets with metal trimmings.

Unfortunately for many teenagers, the black leather jacket became a symbol of

Teenagers also made their own statement in fashions

juvenile delinquency to members of the older generation in the 1950s. The boy who wore such a jacket seemed to advertise himself as tough, self-centered, uncaring of others, and attracted to crime. At the very least, it symbolized to adults an alienation from the rest of society. Such attitudes may have been fostered by some of the popular books and films of the time. Boys wearing such jackets seemed to remind others of James Dean in *Rebel Without a Cause,* or Marlon Brando in *The Wild One.* While gangs, such as the Fordham Baldies, did exist in some neighborhoods in The Bronx, and the aging housing stock in the southern portion of The Bronx created slum conditions, the description of the tough high school filled with hostile and seemingly uneducable youngsters found in the novel *The Blackboard Jungle* by the Bronx's own Evan Hunter perhaps gave the erroneous impression that almost all high schools were like that and that almost all teenagers acted that way, too.

In reality, the vast majority of teenagers growing up in The Bronx at that time were law-abiding and took full advantage of the myriad of social activities available for them. On Friday nights, for instance, it was not unusual to see teenage boys and girls cheering from the stands in their school gymnasium rooting for their high school or college basketball team. Teenagers might also get together at evening dances at their school, church or synagogue, or community center. Saturday night dates at the movies were often topped off by a visit to a ice cream parlor, such as Krum's on the Grand Concourse and 188th Street, Jahn's on Kingsbridge Road near Fordham Road, or Addie Vallins on 161st Street near River Avenue. Even after school, teenagers would often gather around one of the many local pizzerias which seemed to open up in almost every neighborhood throughout the 1950s to munch on steaming hot wedge-shaped slices of pizza topped by melted cheese, anchovies, sausages, or peppers.

Shopping for goods was easy in The Bronx because stores abounded in the neighborhoods. If local army and navy stores or small dress shops on the local neighborhood shopping streets, such as Tremont Avenue, 170th Street, 204th Street, Westchester Square, or 138th Street, did not carry whatever the customer wanted, certainly the department stores would. The most celebrated department store was Alexander's on the northwest corner of the Grand Concourse and Fordham Road, and its original facility on Third Avenue at 153rd Street near the Hub. In both locations, crowds regularly mobbed the main floor and the basement looking through racks and rummaging through drawers beneath large display banquettes seeking bargains. Hearn's at the Hub was also popular, as was Macy's branch store in Parkchester. Roger's Department Store at the southeast corner of Fordham Road and Third Avenue was taken over by the Sear's Roebuck chain to continue a tradition of sales at that location. Loehmann's, the discount women's dress outlet on Fordham Road just west of Jerome Avenue, attracted people from all over The Bronx to seek garments made by expensive manufacturers, but on sale at reasonable prices.

In the 1950s, perhaps the greatest single acquisition desired by a family, was a car. Not only was a car a different means of transportation from the old trolley, bus, and subway, but it was also very personal and a status symbol. It meant the driver had enough money to afford to buy the automobile, and he could now have access to places not easily served by public transportation.

Moreover, cars, in the mid-1950s, were designed to appeal to the eye and the

The most celebrated department store was Alexander's

desire for speed. They ceased to have a boxy shape and were made to look longer, lower, and more streamlined. Automatic transmission made driving easier by eliminating the use of the clutch. The cars also came in a variety of colors, some with two or three tones, including shocking pink. Front windshields wrapped around to the side of the car, and tailfins appeared to grow longer and higher with each succeeding model year. Engines were designed to start quicker and go faster than the legal speed limit.

More cars were sold each year. Since apartments and most private homes had been built without garages, most families parked their cars by the curbside in the street. Generally, there was no great difficulty finding a parking space not too far from home, but, as ownership and traffic increased, so did the number of cars parked along the streets, and a wall of cars parked, and sometimes double parked, along the length of almost every curbside became normal.

On a summer day, a group of people might set off in a family car for Orchard Beach in Pelham Bay Park to spend the day in the sun on the white, creamy-colored sands, with an occasional dip in the waters of Long Island Sound. Others might head for Shorehaven Beach Club at the foot of Soundview Avenue, or Castle Hill Beach Club at the end of Castle Hill Avenue by car and park in their parking lots, although these places were accessible by bus as well. There, the pool beckoned, along with a variety of sports facilities, including handball, tennis, paddleball, basketball, shuffleboard, and baseball. Live entertainment was usually featured every afternoon along with food counters, and a great sense of security.

At night, the car made access to the Whitestone Drive-In Theatre, near the Bronx-Whitestone Bridge, possible. After paying admission for each passenger, the car would be driven into a huge open parking lot. At the head of each parking space was a bump or small hill upon which the two front wheels of the car would rest for easy viewing of the giant screen which formed the wall toward which the car faced. A speaker resting on a metal stand was located to the left of each car. The detachable speaker could be hooked on one of the windows so that the passengers could hear the movie. Movies at this drive-in became available for winter viewing when the management subsequently installed portable heaters for the cars. At any season, however, more interest was often concentrated on what was happening in the back seats of some of the cars, rather than on the screen.

In the early 1960s, Freedomland, the largest amusement park in the world, opened on a previously inaccessible site in the northeast Bronx. Those with cars could make the journey there in a fraction of the time of those traveling by bus. The theme of the park was the history of the United States, and all the pavilions and activities related to that. The visitor would enter walking down "Old New York," an imaginative replica of a shopping street in the early nineteenth century city, whose shops were filled with modern merchandise. A small train pulled by a locomotive circled the grounds, and a horsecar drove people near the center of the grounds to witness the Chicago fire. Every fifteen minutes, flames from gas jets would burst through the windows of a Hollywood cutout building, and spectators would be invited to man the hand-pump fire engine and hose to douse the inferno. The flames, of course, abated on cue, only to reappear fifteen minutes later. Further west, visitors were given the opportunity to descend into the Grand Canyon on a donkey. Although not without interest, Freedomland was not really amusing, except perhaps for the Chicago fire. Within two years, it had gone bankrupt, partly

Freedomland, the largest amusement park in the world

15

because of competition from the 1964 New York World's Fair in nearby Queens.

The increasing use of cars in The Bronx had a significant effect upon public transportation. There were some complaints that trolley cars, with their fixed rail routes in the middle of the streets, hampered the free flow of traffic when they stopped for passengers, and that they were dangerous for pedestrians who had to dodge automobiles to board the trolleys. Moreover, with the population quickly shifting and filling new neighborhoods, trolley routes could not be changed as quickly as the public demanded. Thus, city officials pushed for their removal and the trolleys were doomed. By 1948, all Bronx-based trolley routes were discontinued and replaced by buses; by 1952, all those which came into The Bronx from Westchester County were similarly replaced. Their tracks were either torn up or simply covered with asphalt.

In 1955, the Third Avenue El was discontinued in Manhattan and torn down. Its structure in The Bronx from the Harlem River to the 149th Street Station was destroyed as well. This had the effect of opening up to the light of day the backyards of apartment houses where the elevated trains had run south of 143rd Street. It also reduced the once mighty Third Avenue El route to a mere shuttle line, moving back and forth between Gun Hill and White Plains Roads in Wakefield along Webster and Third Avenues to 149th Street in the Hub. At the southern terminus, passengers had to use an escalator to transfer to the IRT subway below ground so that they could continue their journey to Manhattan.

A similar fate met the remnant of the Sixth and Ninth Avenue Els which ran as a shuttle between the 167th Street Station on the Jerome-Woodlawn elevated section of the IRT Lexington Avenue subway over the Putnam Bridge spanning the Harlem River to 155th Street and Eighth Avenue and the Polo Grounds in Manhattan. This was a valuable connection as long as baseball was played at the old ball park. After the New York Giants moved to San Francisco, service was discontinued, and the elevated line was subsequently torn down. Thus the Putnam Bridge also disappeared, and the unique tunnel which had carried an elevated line beneath 162nd Street in Highbridge was sealed and abandoned.

The increasing prosperity and gradual inflation also affected the transit fare. In 1948, the once sacred five-cent fare was finally abandoned. It doubled to ten cents, and people had to get used to placing dimes in the subway turnstile slots instead of nickels. By the early 1960s, the subway fare rose to fifteen cents, and a small token had to be purchased to fit into the slot. The buses, however, raised their fare to only thirteen cents, but discontinued the issuance of free transfers between bus routes. Now passengers changing buses had to pay the full fare for each bus, making the system less flexible than before. Since the price of gasoline was cheap, these fare changes proved to be an additional incentive for some Bronx families who traveled a great deal to purchase cars instead of relying on public transportation.

The increased use of cars also led to a change in the landscape of The Bronx. To ease actual and potential congestion on Bronx streets, limited access roads had to be built to speed cars on their way. This led to a new flurry of construction similar to the one at the end of the 1930s. The Bronx River Parkway, for instance, was straightened and extended, and its terminus was moved from the Botanical Garden on Southern Boulevard southward to Soundview. In the 1950s, the Major Deegan Expressway was built from its original end point at the Grand Concourse and 138th Street northward along the Harlem River and through Van Cortlandt Park to con-

By 1948, all Bronx-based trolley routes were discontinued

16

nect with the New York Thruway. From the late 1950s into the early 1960s, the Cross-Bronx Expresssway was constructed from the newly-built Throgs Neck Bridge westward through the relatively empty neighborhoods of the eastern half of the borough and the more densely populated apartment house neighborhoods to the west to connect with Manhattan and New Jersey over the new Alexander Hamilton Bridge and the George Washington Bridge. Meanwhile, the New England Thruway came down from Westchester County to connect with a planned new Bruckner Expressway and the Cross-Bronx Expressway.

The changes uprooted whole families in the affected neighborhoods, particularly in Tremont, sometimes only after a bitter losing fight to keep their residences from destruction. The new highways, however, provided greater access to the suburbs for those who already had cars. Sundays could now be spent in Rye's Playland amusement park, or having dinner at Patricia Murphy's restaurant in Yonkers, or out at Jones Beach on Long Island, as well as in any place in The Bronx and New York City. Some liked what they saw in the suburbs, and having the financial ability to own their own home, moved out of The Bronx to Westchester County, Queens, Long Island, or New Jersey. They were aided in this aim by the banks that offered cheap mortgage rates for suburban housing, enabling people to obtain property for a small down payment and a small sum to be paid to the bank each month for thirty years. The new highways which crossed the borough, combined with the new toll bridges, such as the Henry Hudson Bridge to Manhattan, the Triborough Bridge to Manhattan and Queens, and the Bronx-Whitestone, and Throgs Neck Bridges to Queens, meant that those who moved to the suburbs could whisk their way through The Bronx without stopping or seeing the streets or the inhabitants there. For these people, The Bronx became merely a place to pass through at high speed from home to work. They may have retained fond memories of their life in The Bronx, but they were no longer concerned about its future.

Yet, The Bronx continued to have its attractions. Each year, hundreds of thousands of Bronxites were joined by visitors from the metropolitan area and tourists at the Bronx Zoo. People wandered through the grounds watching the monkeys cavort, the elk nibble on the grass, and the seals dive for fish at feeding time. When the zoo displayed the Australian duck-billed platypus in the 1940s, crowds gathered by the deep pool constructed for the creatures to marvel at the unusual combination of a fur-bearing, egg-laying creature with webbed feet and a bill.

... the Edgar Allan Poe Cottage in Poe Park

The New York Botanical Garden to the north of the zoo proved to a be a pleasant place to get away from the pressure of city life. In the midst of flower-covered hillsides and large and sometimes unusual full-leaved trees, it was difficult for a person to remember that he was in the midst of a city.

In fact, rowing on the lakes in Van Cortlandt Park or Crotona Park, or fishing off the rocks at the shore of Long Island Sound in Pelham Bay Park, gave the same feeling. Other, smaller, parks dotted throughout The Bronx provided similar refuges.

Many a Bronx resident visited the past by entering the Van Cortlandt House in Van Cortlandt Park. There, they could admire the colonial furnishings with which the structure was filled. Others would go to the Edgar Allan Poe Cottage in Poe Park at Kingsbridge Road and the Grand Concourse. Here, the furnishings reflected the poverty of the famed nineteenth century poet and author.

The greatest attraction, by far, however, was Yankee Stadium. The great baseball field at River Avenue and 161st Street was a mecca for any fan. The New York Yankees regularly kept winning pennants and World Series, and, perhaps, could not help it considering the talent on the club. From the late 1930s, when the Yankees were led by Lou Gehrig, through the 1940s, the heyday of Joe DiMaggio, through to the 1950s and the dominance of Mickey Mantle, and capped off by the 1961 season when Roger Maris broke Babe Ruth's single season home run record with his sixty-first home run, the Bronx Bombers, as they were nicknamed, dominated the sport. For many years, Yankee players from out of town often stayed at the Concourse Plaza Hotel, nearby on the Grand Concourse, and visiting clubs regularly booked rooms there when they had to play the feared Bombers. At World Series time in October, it was natural to expect avid fans, camping out on the street every night under the elevated subway on River Avenue next to the bleacher entrance, waiting for the tickets to go on sale.

Yankee Stadium was known for more than just baseball, of course. Championship boxing matches such as the 1938 bout between Joe Louis and Max Schmeling, were staged in the ball park, and the New York Football Giants played there when they moved from the Polo Grounds. In addition, starting in the 1950s, the Jehovah's Witnesses took over the stadium for religious purposes for about a week every summer, and in 1965, Pope Paul VI celebrated Mass there as part of his visit to the United States.

Thus, the persistence of neighborhood life, the recreation found in the parks, the continuation of public transportation use and of moviegoing, and the popularity of such institutions as the Bronx Zoo, the New York Botanical Garden, and Yankee Stadium remained to act as a stabilizing core around which we in The Bronx could absorb the rapid changes in the world surrounding us. The time had now arrived when we should devote some time to celebrating ourselves, to show the world what we were and what we had become.

The first movement in this effort came in 1955 with the establishment of The Bronx County Historical Society. A small group under the leadership of Dr. Theodore Kazimiroff, the Bronx Historian, began the institution and nurtured its growth as it sponsored a series of lectures on the Bronx past, conducted walking, bus, and boat tours of the borough, arranged for speakers to visit schools, established a *Journal*, collected objects and library items, and cooperated in the arrangements for the preservation of the historic Valentine-Varian House at Bainbridge Avenue and Van Cortlandt Avenue East, which was destined to become the new Museum of Bronx History.

The second movement came in 1964, the fiftieth anniversary of the creation of Bronx County. Under Borough President Joseph F. Periconi, the Golden Jubilee was proclaimed. A giant parade marched down the Grand Concourse, with bands from many schools and several floats, all glorifying The Bronx and the life of its people. On the reviewing stand in front of the Bronx County Building stood the Borough President, Mayor Robert F. Wagner, and United States Senator Kenneth Keating. Caught up in the joy of the occasion, Ernest E.L. Hammer, an attorney who had served as the county's first Public Administrator, and who was the last surviving member of the original county government, pranced down the stairs of the reviewing platform and took a place in the line of march, waving merrily in his right hand, back and forth over his head, one of the little, especially-designed blue and white desk-top Bronx Golden Jubilee flags.

The following year, in the election of 1965, the Democrats recaptured control of the Borough President's Office. The new leader of The Bronx was Herman Badillo. This continued the pattern of stability in the midst of change. As in the past, the office reflected the predominant Democratic registration among the people of the borough, but the man newly-elected to the office was a member of the Reform faction of the party, and had been born in Puerto Rico. Thus, his election also pointed toward the future.

Just before the election was held came the unexpected announcement of a plan to build a huge apartment house complex on the site of the defunct Freedomland amusement park. Projected as a series of high rise houses at the edge of the Hutchinson River in an area dominated by single family homes, it was planned to attract middle income people who wanted to own apartments selling at very reasonable prices. The breadth of the vision for the project, at 15,000 apartments, was larger than that of Parkchester, and the Amalgamated Clothing Workers, who sponsored the idea, called it Co-op City. This announcement, too, pointed toward the future.

Yet, so much of the past remains . . .

Yet, so much of the past remains, it seems as if The Bronx of 1935 to 1965 was only yesterday. The people of The Bronx today are still ethnically diverse and still center their lives in their neighborhoods, still value their religious traditions, still shop at Fordham Road and the Hub, still travel the subways and buses, still strive for the best education for their children, still cheer for the New York Yankees, still enjoy visits to the Bronx Zoo, and still relax in the shade of trees in the parks. Indeed, in The Bronx, much of the change, in some respects, has not touched the essential way of life which made the borough such a wonderful place in which to grow up and in which to live during the middle of the twentieth century. Certainly, there have been changes, but all the essential advantages The Bronx afforded its people, and the basic values which the people held then, are still alive in today's Bronx. Thus, the passing decades seem only to have been a moment, and The Bronx of yesterday still persists in The Bronx of today.

From Subway to Highway

A NORTHBOUND TRAIN OF THE BROADWAY SEVENTH AVENUE SUBWAY LINE crosses the Broadway Bridge over the Harlem River Ship Canal in the fall of 1960. The center of the bridge rests on a pivot mechanism that swings the bridge around parallel to the waterway to allow passage of tall ships. In the background to the left rises the tall building of the Kingsbridge Veterans Administration Hospital.

AT THE HUB, THIRD AVENUE AND 149TH STREET,
commuters on the platform await the arrival of an uptown Third
Avenue El train in 1949. Below the elevated structure are some of the
specialty shops that made the Hub a shopper's mecca. A Thom McAn
shoe store and a Howard's clothing shop flank a small bar and grill.
A bus, with its familiar red and cream colors, and its slogan
"Ride the Surface Way" written above the side windows, waits
at a public restroom on the traffic island to the right.

DISPATCHER EMIL DAMSEAUX talks with the engineer on a train
alongside the Morris Park Avenue platform of the East 180th Street IRT
subway station in 1956. This is where subway trains headed northward
along White Plains Road and the trains of the northbound
Dyre Avenue Line diverge.

THE MARBLE HILL STATION of the New York Central Railroad's
Hudson division stood to the east of Broadway in the fall of 1960.
To the left, a Circle Line sightseeing boat sailing around Manhattan
makes the turn from the Harlem River into the Harlem River
Ship Canal. The highrise Fordham Hill Apartments punctuate
the skyline to the left.

TREMONT AVENUE NEAR BRUCKNER BOULEVARD, in 1947, was the location of the terminus of the Tremont Avenue trolley. The tracks embedded in the street west of Bruckner Boulevard afforded an opportunity for the trolleys to cross the tracks prior to their return journey. The trolley has just completed the crossover and has yet to lower the pole on its roof that connected the car to the elevated power supply from the wires overhead. That pole was used for the eastbound trip, while a pole based on the other end of the roof would be raised for the westbound journey.
The interchange was a center of local commerce;
an office of The Bronx County Trust Company is seen
on the near corner to the left.

The Bronx County Historical Society
Research Library

THE CROSS-BRONX EXPRESSWAY under construction on November 11, 1950. The recessed highway necessitated the erection of a new bridge to carry Castle Hill Avenue over the new highway. Cranes and other construction equipment dwarf the men and their supervisors in the work area.

THE CROSS-BRONX EXPRESSWAY NEAR CASTLE HILL AVENUE in the early 1950s. At this point, the new major highway is depressed below the grade of the streets of the surrounding neighborhood, and a pedestrian bridge has been constructed to allow traffic along the side streets to cross unimpeded. The stone retaining wall and its metal fence is already completed, while work crews are rapidly finishing work on the roadway itself. Much of the surrounding Unionport area seems barely touched by the construction work, including the prominent Tudor style Castillian Gardens apartment house in the center. *The Bronx County Historical Society Research Library*

LOCUST AVENUE SOUTH OF 138TH STREET, in the heavily industrialized Port Morris section, is the scene of the removal of the old trolley tracks around 1950. A worker from the Harlem Metal Corporation, which, despite its name, is headquartered nearby at 135th Street in The Bronx, is using an acetylene torch to cut the now raised tracks into smaller strips, while a truck behind him to the right straddles the tracks bearing a mechanism to rip the metal from the roadway and roll it up. The roll will then be shipped to the company as scrap metal. The large brick industrial building in the center is the huge factory of the R. Hoe Company, world-famous manufacturers of printing presses.

The Bronx County Historical Society Research Library

BAYCHESTER AVENUE NEAR BOSTON ROAD is receiving a new
road surface around 1950. The construction crew has already run
sticky black tar over half the Belgian block in the street and are in
the process of spreading over it some gravel carried in their shovels
from a pile. The area has many empty lots interspersed with
single family homes.

The Bronx County Historical Society
Research Library

BRONX PARK EAST AND ALLERTON AVENUE about 1948 was the center of the reconstruction of the Bronx River Parkway through Bronx Park. The roadway connecting Allerton Avenue to the right with Mosholu Parkway on the other side of the park is being remade to flow under a new overpass carrying the Bronx River Parkway. In the background in the center at the tops of the trees, a straight, dark line is really the Third Avenue El along Webster Avenue. The structures on the horizon to the right mark the Norwood, Kingsbridge Heights, and Riverdale neighborhoods.

THE RAILROAD YARDS SOUTH OF THE HIGH BRIDGE in 1958 is a scene showing the old and the new. The men are standing on the site where the old New York Central Putnam Division Railroad tracks used to rest before they were taken up. To the left is a locomotive and caboose on the Hudson Division tracks at the Highbridge station. The overpass just over the heads of the men is Depot Place. Rising above it are the graceful rounded stone arches of the High Bridge itself. Midway through the arches in the right center can be seen a new structure marking the beginning of construction of the Alexander Hamilton Bridge that will take the new Cross-Bronx Expressway over the Harlem River to Manhattan. Beyond that can be seen the metal latticework of the Washington Bridge that takes traffic from The Bronx to Manhattan's West 181st Street. *The Bronx County Historical Society Research Library–Seifert Collection*

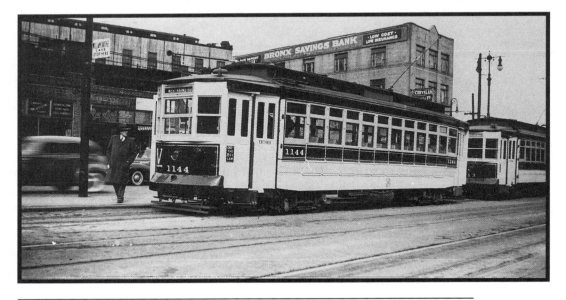

The Bronx County Historical Society Research Library

WEST FARMS SQUARE about 1940 was a busy transportation hub as many trolley lines converged there. A man is waiting on the pedestrian traffic island where the cars from Williamsbridge end their run and begin the return journey. The letter "V" in the front of the car to the left signals to anyone at a distance that this trolley car is the Williamsbridge Road Line. Across the street to the left are local shops, while the small office building behind the trolleys to the right bears an outdoor sign advertising the Bronx Savings Bank, which also sells low cost life insurance.

St. Ann's Avenue at Its Junction with Third Avenue is where the St. Anns Avenue trolley line, marked with the letter "L" in front, begins its run in the mid-1930s. The shadow of the Third Avenue El to the left is cast over the waiting trolley car, but does not reach the four-story apartment houses in the center and to the left. Some tenants have awnings over the windows to lower the heat generated by the sun. Others have their window shades drawn. At the street level, shops, such as a hardware store and a pharmacy, cater to the residents of the neighborhood. *The Bronx County Historical Society Research Library*

Broadway and 230th Street is the scene of a fatal subway accident on September 26, 1957. Movement on this elevated portion of the Broadway-Seventh Avenue line of the subway had to be halted as firemen prevent the spread of flame. Subway crews man a crane and take care of injured passengers from the head-on collision in which the motorman, Mr. Timberlake, was killed.

The Bronx County Historical Society Research Library
–Bessie Wherry Noe, photographer

135TH STREET NEAR WILLOW AVENUE in Port Morris is practically deserted on a summer morning in 1935. The recently completed elevated approach to the new Triborough Bridge dominates the scene. Behind the Chevrolet sign, strategically placed so that motorists using the approach can easily see it, is the Jacob Doll and Sons Piano Factory.   *The Bronx County Historical Society Research Library*

138TH STREET AT THE FOOT OF THE GRAND CONCOURSE in 1935 is the site of the newly-built overpass that takes motorists onto the recently completed Major Deegan Expressway to the Triborough Bridge. On the piers on either side of 138th Street, a concrete block juts out bearing the seal of the borough of The Bronx. A new park with recently-planted trees occupies the foreground, and is fenced off from the sidewalk. To the left, a number 1 Concourse bus has just finished its run. Under the arch, across 138th Street, is the entrance to the Mott Haven station of the Lexington Avenue subway, while further to the right, partially hidden by the pier, is the Mott Haven station of the New York Central Railroad.   *The Bronx County Historical Society Research Library*

UNIONPORT ROAD NEAR TREMONT AVENUE in the Morris Park neighborhood bears a rural atmosphere in 1938. The lots in the front and to the left are divided into small farms, while the large structure beyond them marks a tavern and beer garden. Behind the beer garden is the steel signal support for the New York, New Haven, and Hartford Railroad. To the right of the billboards in the center advertising Pittsburgh Paints and Chevrolet automobiles is the storage silo of the Starck-Rawlins Coal Company on Tremont Avenue.

HUGH GRANT CIRCLE AT 177TH STREET in October, 1938 is dominated by the elevated station of the Lexington Avenue local line. Pedestrians can walk freely into the roadway without being overly vigilant for passing automobiles. In fact, there are only three cars in the photograph. To the lower left are some local shops, including a grocery store. A vacant lot to the right sports advertising billboards. Beyond the elevated structure rises the first houses of Parkchester to be completed.

The Bronx County Historical Society Research Library

The Bronx County Historical Society Research Library –Schleissman Collection

AT THE MERGE OF THE THROGS NECK EXPRESSWAY AND THE BRUCKNER EXPRESSWAY in 1965 is the spire of the First Lutheran Church in the center on Baisley Avenue. Cars are parked along the curbside of Hollywood Avenue to the left.

OGDEN AVENUE AT THE INTERSECTION OF JEROME AVENUE is the scene
of many changes in 1950. The traffic island in the middle of Jerome
Avenue bearing the streetlight and the movable traffic signs instructing the
few passing motorists to keep right is new, and the roadway is made of
newly-poured asphalt. The new material covers the old trolley tracks that
can still be seen in the middle of the roadway of the Ogden Avenue hill.
Along the curb on the sidewalk of Ogden Avenue, new trees have been
planted, while older trees in the parks on either side of Ogden Avenue rise
much higher. Toward the top of the Ogden Avenue hill are some of the
apartment houses where residents of this Highbridge neighborhood reside.
Their cars are parked along the curb near the houses, but there are
plenty of spaces closer to the base of the hill.

THE END OF CLASON POINT in the early 1950s is the scene of the abandoned Clason Point ferry slips. Until the construction of the Bronx-Whitestone Bridge, passengers, many in motor cars, used to crowd the ferries anchored in these slips to travel to Queens. With grass and weeds growing wild, the only activity in sight is an automobile parked near Kaiser's Boat House, which advertises that it has beer on tap.

The Bronx County Historical Society Research Library–Schleissman Collection

The Bronx County Historical Society Research Library

FORDHAM ROAD AT UNIVERSITY AVENUE is an active trolley car stop in 1946. The Bailey Avenue car, marked by the "B" in the front, is on its way to Fordham Square at Third Avenue. People have no fear of traffic as they cross the street or wait for the trolley in the middle of the roadway paved with Belgian block. Other residents sit at the benches along the sidewalk at Devoe Park across the street.

FORDHAM ROAD NEAR HAMPDEN PLACE LOOKING WESTWARD TOWARD CEDAR AVENUE in February, 1952, shows its old Belgian block roadway being covered with asphalt. Several cars are parked along the curb to the left near the six-story apartment house with shops at street level. Those shops include a Chinese hand laundry, a dry cleaner, a tavern, and a luncheonette. Across Cedar Avenue is a Mobil service station. Beyond it and the single-story structure with a sign advertising Walter B. Cooke's funeral parlors on the roof is the University Heights station of the New York Central Railroad's Hudson line. Just below the crane near the station a Fordham Road bus can be seen coming from Manhattan exiting from the University Heights Bridge that crosses the Harlem River. To the right is the showroom of Dale Oldsmobile.   *The Bronx County Historical Society Research Library*

FORDHAM ROAD AT LORING PLACE looking west is still predominantly paved in Belgian block. But by the early 1950s, the old trolley tracks are partially covered by asphalt. Apartment houses, a Gulf Oil station, and the Tolentine Diner occupy the block to the left, while Devoe Park across the street to the right is used by neighborhood residents. Behind the park on the corner of Sedgwick Avenue rises the frame of a large gas tank.   *The Bronx County Historical Society Research Library*

FORDHAM ROAD AND SEDGWICK AVENUE in 1952 is in the process of having its Belgian block roadway repaved with new asphalt. Passing traffic is confined to narrow paths to the left and the right of the area the steamroller in the center is working on. Devoe Park is found to the left, while the line of apartment houses to the right is broken by a Gulf service station. Portions of the roofs of the buildings are studded with new television antennas, while the side of one building bears an outdoor advertisement for RCA Victor television service. At the street level, there are stores catering to the residents of this neighborhood near the western end of Fordham Road, including a cleaner and dyer, a luncheonette, an appliance repair shop, a wine and liquor store, a grocery, a meat market, and a fruit and vegetable store.

The Bronx County Historical Society Research Library

FORDHAM ROAD NEAR WEBSTER AVENUE in 1952 is having its new asphalt roadway smoothed by steamrollers. Some of the rubble from the reconstruction is piled along the sidewalk near the curb to the right, and crowds of people attracted to the shopping along this major retail center try to navigate along the remaining space. The park at Fordham Square, with its prominent restroom, is to the left. In the center is the entrance to the Fordham Station serving the Harlem Division of The New York Central Railroad. In front of it are two buses picking up passengers. Above them is the Fordham station of the Third Avenue El.

Boston Road Looking South from the Intersection of Ropes Avenue in the northeastern corner of The Bronx is a Belgian block roadway, partially covered with asphalt, and flanked by low-lying buildings, most of which are industrial or commercial. In July, 1965, an exception is the Wedge Inn to the center left, a luncheonette specializing in sandwiches catering to the workers in the surrounding establishments. A circular sign on the sidewalk to the right advises visiting businessmen coming into The Bronx from Westchester County that the Bronx Lions Club meets Wednesdays at noon at the Concourse Plaza Hotel.   *The Bronx County Historical Society Research Library*

The Bronx County Historical Society
Research Library

Bedford Park Boulevard at the Intersection of Decatur Avenue in 1950 boasts of a five-story apartment house to the right, with shops at the street level, and older, late nineteenth century three-story structures to the left, which also have street level stores. The wide thoroughfare is a local shopping street, dominated by the Bedford Park Boulevard station of the Third Avenue El over Webster Avenue in the center.

THE MAJOR DEEGAN EXPRESSWAY AT WILLIS AVENUE
as seen from the nearby Third Avenue El station in the
late 1930s shows very few cars on either the new highway
or on the overpass built to take Willis Avenue over it.
In fact, there are more passengers on the trolley car to
the left than in the cars seen in the photograph. Saplings
dot the hills sloping toward the expressway. Many of the
tenants in the apartments houses along 135th Street
paralleling the highway to the left have their awnings
drawn to keep the harsh sunlight and the heat away from
their windows, something not needed by the tenants in
the houses along 134th Street to the right. In the
distance rise the industrial buildings of Port Morris,
while the vista along the highway ends in a prominent
billboard advertising Schaefer Beer.

The Bronx County Historical Society Research Library

JEROME AVENUE AT 176TH STREET in 1939 is dominated by the 176th Street elevated station of the Lexington
Avenue subway's Woodlawn-Jerome line. The light
traffic navigates its way amid the elevated pillars. A taxi,
parked dangerously close to a fire hydrant, waits for a fare
at the base of the subway's stairs. The truck to the right
is from Arnold and Beckmann, distributors of McKay
bottled milk. To the left can be seen the sign of the De
Luxe Restaurant hanging over the street. To the extreme
right is a mailbox attached to a lamppost, next to which
is a metal box standing on the sidewalk, where full mail
sacks are delivered and picked up by passing mailmen
on their routes.

The Bronx County Historical Society Research Library

BRUCKNER BOULEVARD AT LONGFELLOW AVENUE has moderate traffic in the late 1940s. The wide thoroughfare is flanked by a school and playground to the right and by service stations to the left. Beyond the service stations are the sunken railroad tracks of the New York, New Haven and Hartford Railroad's freight line. The apartment houses beyond it to the left form part of the Hunts Point neighborhood. The large building with the tower piercing the skyline to the center is the American Bank Note Company's printing plant in Hunts Point.

THE BRONX ENTRANCE TO THE TRIBOROUGH BRIDGE AT THE FOOT OF CYPRESS AVENUE in 1935. The new facility is marked by a sign informing motorists that they have to pay a toll on the bridge taking them to Queens, Manhattan, Long Island, or Randall's Island.

The Bronx County Historical Society
Research Library

THE BRONX RIVER NEAR 233RD STREET forms a peaceful winter scene in the
early 1960s. Traffic streams along the Bronx River Parkway to the right, while
the Harlem Division railroad tracks occupy the hill above the riverbank to the left.
The switching tower is near the center of the photograph. The new apartment
house buildings, some with exterior terraces, on the horizon to the left form
the eastern edge of the Woodlawn Heights neighborhood.

The Bronx County Historical Society
Research Library

BRUCKNER BOULEVARD AT WESTCHESTER CREEK is being widened in the mid-1940s. Workmen across the water at the border of the Castle Hill neighborhood are preparing a slope that will eventually support a bridge that will carry the thoroughfare across to Throggs Neck. Anchored in the creek on either shore to the left are houseboats.

The Bronx County Historical Society
Research Library

Going
Shopping

The Bronx County Historical Society
Research Library

FORDHAM ROAD AND VALENTINE AVENUE in 1952 is the home of the RKO Fordham Theater. Its marquee boasts that this is the first day for the new double feature, "I'll Never Forget You," starring Tyrone Power and Ann Blythe, and "Girl on the Bridge," starring Beverly Michaels. To the left of the theater are a men's store, a Fanny Farmer candy store, Albrecht's dress shop, Benhill shoe store, and London shoe store. In the center rises Alexander's Department Store, with its motto, "Uptown it's Alexanders," on a huge sign on its roof. To the left is a number 12 Fordham Road crosstown bus.

ON THE SOUTHWEST CORNER OF FORDHAM ROAD AND VALENTINE AVENUE in the mid-1960s stands the two-story Hagedorn Building. Above the Woolworth's five and ten cent store, the Lerner's dress shop, and the Simco shoe store are offices for two brokerage firms and the Beneficial Loan Company. The entire edifice is topped by a billboard advertising Schenley whiskey. To the right is the Art Deco style Wagner Building. On the street level can be seen the Brighton Cafeteria. The traffic light is extended over the intersection by a stanchion at the corner, which also bears a new "Walk-Don't Walk" sign for pedestrians. Nearby, on Valentine Avenue at the curb, stands three new public telephone booths.

The Bronx County Historical Society Research Library

FORDHAM ROAD AND VALENTINE AVENUE is at the center of the major shopping street in The Bronx in 1951. Cars, trucks, and a bus use the roadway, while shoppers cram the sidewalks to patronize such concerns as Gorman's frankfurter and drinks, Whelan's Drug Store, Howard Clothes, A.S. Beck Shoe Store, Bond's Clothes, Ripley's Clothes, Adler's Shoes, and Roger's Department Store to the right. Across the street are Madow's jewelers, an Automat, and Bostonian Shoes. The Gothic tower of Keating Hall on the Fordham University campus rises in the center.

The Bronx County Historical Society Research Library

235TH STREET AT THE INTERSECTION OF JOHNSON AVENUE in Spuyten Duyvil is a local shopping center for residents in the apartment houses and the single family homes. The taxpayer provides a luncheonette, Solomon's Liquor Store, an air conditioned drug store, Travers Cleaners and Tailors, and a Peter Reeves supermarket, which sells bread for fifteen cents a loaf in the 1950s.

A taxpayer is a one or two story building constructed with space for stores with the aim to produce enough revenue to pay its taxes.

PROSPECT AVENUE AT THE INTERSECTION OF 187TH STREET in the mid-1950s shows clear signs that this is
a predominantly Italian neighborhood. At the corner to the right is the Colavolpe Brothers pastry shop
(*pasticceria* in Italian), specializing in wedding and birthday cakes, but also offering Italian varieties of ice cream.
On the opposite corner to the left is a Whelan's drug store. Apartment houses dominate both corners and the
right side of Prospect Avenue, while town houses can be found in the middle of the block to the left.
The windows of the apartment house to the right all bear Venetian blinds. Although cars occupy every
parking space at the curbs, traffic is relatively light enough to permit some boys to ride their
bicycles in the roadway of Prospect Avenue. *The Bronx County Historical Society Research Library–Max Levine Collection*

TREMONT AVENUE WEST OF WESTCHESTER SQUARE is an area filled with local shops in the 1950s.
The string of stores to the center and left, decorated with red, white, and blue bunting, has just opened for
business, joining an older A & P Supermarket to the right. *The Bronx County Historical Society Research Library*

SOUTHEAST CORNER OF BROOK AVENUE AND 138TH STREET in the 1940s, holds a three-story building with shops at the street level and a billiard parlor on the second floor. The Forum Liquor Store at 225 Brook Avenue sports a neon sign pointing customers to the entrance. The Mayaguez Shoe Store to the right is one of the first shops operated by a Puerto Rican.

ON WESTCHESTER SQUARE, a Kenmar shop celebrates its grand opening in the 1950s. Its dresses, blouses, skirts, and accessories are displayed in the window to entice women to buy them. A free gift for every purchase is advertised as an added inducement, and one sign in the window states that charge accounts are welcome. On the sidewalk in front of the shop is a parking meter that limits shoppers coming by automobile to only sixty minutes of parking.

The Bronx County Historical Society
Research Library
—Max Levine Collection

165TH STREET AT THE CORNER OF MORRIS AVENUE in the 1950s is a local shopping area, including a repair shop for the new television sets that people in the neighborhood are increasingly buying. The tall structure to the right houses the Fleetwood Theater, which shows movies that had already been seen in first, second, and third-run theaters. Cars are parked along 165th Street, while a lone woman waits in the bus stop for the northbound Morris Avenue bus. Morris Avenue is paved with red brick.

The Bronx County Historical Society Research Library–Max Levine Collection

WASHINGTON AVENUE NEAR TREMONT AVENUE in the 1950s is dominated by thriving shops. They include a Chinese restaurant, whose main entrance lies around the corner on Tremont Avenue, a barber shop, a jeweler, an electric and radio shop, a Woolworth five and ten cent store, an egg store, and a printing shop. Above them to the right is a music school, while the upstairs space to the left is vacant. The building to the left is the A. Santini moving and storage warehouse. On the horizon is the spire of St. Joseph's Church. Two-way traffic on Washington Avenue is congested with cars parked at the curb and a taxi and passenger cars trying to find their way through.

The Bronx County Historical Society Research Library –Max Levine Collection

THE CORNER OF KINGSBRIDGE ROAD AND VALENTINE AVENUE in 1960 is the site of a taxpayer structure that hugs the rounded corner of the intersection. The luncheonette and Dora's Gown Shoppe (which boasts that it has air conditioning) sport Kingsbridge Road addresses, while Cardinal's Pharmacy, the neighboring vacant store, Matt's delicatessen, and a local supermarket are all on Valentine Avenue. Apartment houses facing Valentine Avenue and the Grand Concourse rise above the smaller structure. At the corner, a truck bearing cases of Hoffman's sodas is making a delivery. *The Bronx County Historical Society Research Library–Max Levine Collection*

KINGSBRIDGE ROAD JUST TO THE WEST OF JEROME AVENUE in December, 1952, is the site of several local shops in a taxpayer structure. These include a barber shop, an upholsterer, a furrier, a hardware store, a beautician's supply shop, and Fitzgerald's tavern and restaurant. Rising above Jerome Avenue is the Kingsbridge Road station of the Lexington Avenue subway's Woodlawn-Jerome express line. At the corner is a bus stop, while a bus can be seen diagonally across the street in the stop servicing those who wish to go westward. Beyond, in the center of the photograph, is the marquee of the Kingsbridge Theater advertising the current double feature film presentation. Traffic is moving freely along Kingsbridge Road, but it is filled with trucks and cars. *The Bronx County Historical Society Research Library*

The Bronx County Historical Society
Research Library

MELROSE AVENUE AT 150TH STREET in the late 1950s is the site
of a new three-story commercial building at the busy Hub section of The
Bronx. Offices occupy the top two floors and sport new aluminum
casement windows, while the tenants keep out the harsh sunlight with
Venetian blinds. On the street level, the stores are occupied by Cushman's
bakery, Joe's Army and Navy Store, Lynn's clothing store, and Peter's
florist. Taller office buildings hem in the newer structure.
Cars crowd out all available parking spaces at the curb, while asphalt
partially covers the Belgian block and old trolley tracks
in the roadway.

THE CORNER OF GUN HILL AND EASTCHESTER ROADS is the site of the
farm stand of the Russell family in 1941. Here, they are selling Long Island
potatoes and sweet apple cider. Much of their produce and cider jugs are
displayed along the curb, while more is stored in the shed to the left, where
apples, onions, and corn are also available. A few neighborhood families
are inspecting some of the displays.

The Bronx County Historical Society
Research Library
–Mary Russell Collection

STUDENTS FROM LOCAL SCHOOLS walk along Castle Hill Avenue between Haviland and Powell Avenues in 1947. The street is lined with small local shops, including a barber shop with its distinctive striped pole in front of the window; farther down the street is the Garofalo Beauty Salon. In the distance is the elevated Castle Hill Avenue station of the IRT Lexington Avenue local subway. *The Bronx County Historical Society Research Library*

163RD STREET NEAR WESTCHESTER AVENUE is a thriving neighborhood shopping center serving a growing Puerto Rican population in 1949. Next to the candy store on the right, with its newspapers inside and its sign advertising Mission Orange Soda is the Palmer Drug Store with its new sign in Spanish hanging over the street. Next door is the Morales travel agency, with its signs written in both languages. The elevated structure of the Lexington and Seventh Avenue White Plains Road subway lines rise high above Westchester Avenue. *The Bronx County Historical Society Research Library*

Tremont Avenue at the Corner of Washington Avenue in the 1950s
has a two-story commercial structure built in the Art Deco style of the
1930s. At street level, from left to right, is a butcher store that sells poultry parts,
a tuxedo shop, a Chinese restaurant that displays a banner over its window
advertising that it is air conditioned, an optometrist, and F.W. Woolworth's
five and ten cent store. Above is a music school and a dance studio.
At the corner, a new bus stop sign is installed, even though the old trolley
tracks in the center of the street still remain.

*The Bronx County Historical Society
Research Library*

THE GRAND CONCOURSE AT 183RD STREET is near the southern end of the shopping district centering on Fordham Road to the north in the mid-1950s. On the northwestern corner of the intersection, a taxpayer, built in the 1930s, houses Sullivan's Bar and Grill, a decorator's shop with objects of art, several apparel shops, a candy store, a book shop, and the Ascot, a small theater that usually screens foreign films. To the right of the Ascot is the Concourse Center of Israel synagogue.

The Bronx County Historical Society Research Library–Max Levine Collection

AT TREMONT AVENUE WEST OF WESTCHESTER SQUARE stands the Pape Chevrolet showroom. The salesmen are gathered on the sidewalk to inspect a new 1960 model car that has just arrived. The showroom window proclaims the various models of Chevrolets that are available to the increasing number of Bronx residents who want to own cars.

The Bronx County Historical Society Research Library

WHITE PLAINS ROAD AT THE INTERSECTION WITH BRUCKNER BOULEVARD
is easy for pedestrians to cross about 1956, despite the presence of heavy
trucks. The Korvette's shopping center, one of the first suburban-type shopping
centers in The Bronx is located behind the truck and to the right, with its
parking lot filled with cars. The Robin Hood stand to the left sells
cheeseburgers and hot dogs for twenty-five cents each.

149TH STREET AT CALDWELL AVENUE is dominated by a large rock outcropping in March, 1954. Hugging the base of the rock is Murray S. Paroly's used car dealership. He provides his customers with a ninety day guarantee, and will accept old cars in trade. His motto, "Better Cars for Better Driving," is printed prominently below his name on the sign. Above his small lot are apartment houses that can be reached by climbing up a long staircase from the street. A woman pushing a shopping cart in front of her is trying to cross the bumpy Belgian block paving of 149th Street. The whole streetcorner is slated to be changed because the man in the middle of the street holding the sign with the legend "P80" is assisting surveyors planning to build the St. Mary's Park public housing project on the site.

The Bronx County Historical Society Research Library

PARKWAY PHOTOGRAPHERS AT FORDHAM ROAD NEAR WASHINGTON AVENUE in 1955 is a major photographic studio in The Bronx, specializing in portraits and recording social and political functions. Its proprietor, Max Levine, is adjusting the display on his counter.

The Bronx County Historical Society Research Library–Max Levine Collection

Industry
and
Commerce

*The Bronx County Historical Society
Research Library*

JUST SOUTH OF 149TH STREET BETWEEN RIVER AND GERARD AVENUES in 1939 lies an extensive lumberyard located in a neighborhood filled with factories and warehouses. Exterior Street angles off River Avenue to the left. At the extreme left at the corner is part of the Erie Railroad freight station. Across the street, the triangular building is the extension of the Bronx Terminal Market. The tall, white structure piercing the roofline at the northern end of the market is the Bronx County Jail. Behind it, and partially hidden by it, is Yankee Stadium. Traffic on River Avenue and Gerard Avenue, including several taxicabs, are streaming northward toward the stadium for a game. Beyond the empty lots in the center are the five- and six-story apartment houses of the Grand Concourse neighborhood. Piercing the skyline to the right are the cube-shaped Bronx County Building and the Concourse Plaza Hotel.

ALONG 161ST STREET EAST OF WALTON AVENUE in October, 1950, officials from the Surface Transit System participate in a ceremony displaying sixty new buses and three radio patrol cars to be used in The Bronx. At the wheel of the car, using its telephone, is Bronx Borough President James J. Lyons. Behind the buses to the left rises the Bronx County Building, while the apartment houses on Walton Avenue can be seen to the right.

The Bronx County Historical Society
Research Library
—Joseph Duffy Collection

THE KINGSBRIDGE VETERANS HOSPITAL AT KINGSBRIDGE ROAD AND SEDGWICK AVENUE was a busy place during and after World War II. This, the only federally-run hospital in The Bronx, treated soldiers for the physical and mental effects of the conflict in a multi-storied red-brick complex amid a broad tree-filled and grass-covered campus setting.

The Bronx County Historical Society Research Library

BRONX BOULEVARD JUST NORTH OF 237TH STREET in the
Wakefield neighborhood is dominated by an industrial building
topped by a square tower in the 1950s. Across the street to the right
are single family frame residences. The presence of the working
men and the local inhabitants insure that the street, which
has little traffic, is nevertheless filled with parked cars.

ON 149TH STREET NEAR COURTLANDT AVENUE stands an eight story office building, with its street level filled with stores in the 1950s. One is taken by the Commercial State Bank, while the others are occupied by an establishment repairing radios, televisions, and other electric appliances, and a luncheonette. The adjoining buildings to the left house a barber shop, a realtor, and a bar. These structures are also residences for tenants who live above. On the side of the office building is a painted sign directing customers to the Wool Brothers store across the street, which specializes in selling appliances at discount prices.

The Bronx County Historical Society Research Library

ON PROSPECT AVENUE NEAR 162ND STREET stands the Hollywood Clothing store, owned by Elias Karmon, a major businessman in this local shopping street. It specializes in mens' clothing, both ready-to-wear and custom made, but also advertises that it serves women as well. Its wares are tastefully displayed in the window. To the left can be seen part of a radio and record shop, which also used Spanish in its signs to appeal to the growing Puerto Rican presence in the neighborhood. To the right is a Chinese restaurant.

The Bronx County Historical Society Research Library
−Karmon Collection
−John Gardner, photographer

OAK POINT AVENUE NEAR THE END OF TIFFANY STREET in Hunts
Point is the site of the large parking lot of the American Gypsum Company
about 1960. In this largely industrial area, the massive and long building
of the Grand Iron Works, with its entire upper half almost completely
glass, dominates the scene near the center. Yet, a baseball field with its
wire mesh backstop is located there to the left. On the horizon to
the left rise the apartment houses hugging Hunts Point Avenue.

NEAR MILES AVENUE ON MORRIS COVE LEADING TO THE EAST RIVER at Ferry Point stands a boatyard in 1948. Inside the structure are the workbenches and machines needed to build and repair boats. Lumber is stacked on the wall to the center right, while other supplies are placed among the rafters above. Wood chips and shavings litter the floor.

AT 140TH STREET AND THE EAST RIVER IN PORT MORRIS stands the headquarters of the H.O. Penn Machinery Company in 1945. With the increase in the need for heavy construction equipment following World War II, business is picking up. Here, a truck is hauling a crane on a trailer.

West Farms Road near Jennings Street in April, 1948 is the site of the
Weinstock Package Supply Company, which distributes wooden crates to fruit
and vegetable dealers. In the center yard, workmen are taking the stacked crates
and readying them for shipment in trucks. Vehicles make use not only of the
roadway, but of the sidewalk as well.

The Bronx County Historical Society
Research Library

ON WEBSTER AVENUE NEAR 182ND STREET in the 1960s stands the headquarters of the A-A Ambulance and Oxygen Service. The line of new ambulances outside the garage doors stand ready to take anyone who calls to a nearby hospital in an emergency. The firm also rents and sells wheelchairs, hospital beds, sick room equipment, and hospital therapy service. To the right, is the offices of the Tremont branch of Davis and Warshow, which sells plumbing and heating supplies and bathroom appliances.

ON 149TH STREET NEAR PARK AVENUE stands the Fuel Terminal Building, a major office structure, in 1950. Eight floors of offices rise above street-level shops, which include a luncheonette and an auto parts store. Next door, to the left, is a two-story taxpayer with another luncheonette and the headquarters of companies manufacturing construction equipment. The side of the office building is filled with outdoor advertising for the Central Coal Company, Calvert Whiskey, and the Dwight Vooris and Helmsley real estate company.

The Bronx County Historical Society Research Library

THE CORNER OF 233RD STREET AND BUSSING AVENUE sports a busy Esso service station in the midst of a snow storm around 1960. One car waits at a pump to fill up on gas, while another waits in front of the garage area for possible servicing. At the corner to the right, cars are parked in the empty part of the lot, while others are parked at the curb. Tire tracks in the accumulated snow indicate that a number of cars had passed by, but traffic is nonexistent at the time this photograph was taken. Behind the gas station is a row of attached town houses, while a taller apartment building looms over them on the horizon.

Housing

THE PELHAM PARKWAY HOUSES at Bronxwood Avenue and Williamsbridge Road in the Pelham Parkway neighborhood was recently completed in September, 1951, when some of the first residents took their youngsters, baby carriages, and tricycles along the grass-flanked paths with newly-planted trees. They lived in the six-story brick apartment buildings with casement windows designed by the New York City Housing Authority.

ON FISH AVENUE BETWEEN BOSTON ROAD AND HICKS STREET
stands the Hillside Houses. Noted for its siting amid gardens, grass,
and trees, it features apartments facing inner garden courts.
Here, two groups of boys, the older ones wearing football uniforms,
converse in the mid-1960s over a chain link fence along a shaded
concrete walkway far from any automobile traffic.

TREMONT AVENUE AT THE INTERSECTION OF THE GRAND CONCOURSE is almost devoid of traffic in April, 1937. Monroe Avenue, angling off the intersection to the right, forms a triangle with the Grand Concourse upon which rises the ornate Medical Arts Building to the right. One doctor's office at the apex of the triangle on the second floor indicates that the space is for rent. Across Monroe Avenue are four small buildings facing Tremont Avenue. On the corner is Stein's drug store and luncheonette. Further down Monroe Avenue is a two car garage. The adjoining apartment house displays a sign on its side just above the second floor advertising that each apartment is equipped with a General Electric refrigerator. The main roadway of Tremont Avenue is carried below the Grand Concourse in an underpass marked by an iron fence.   *The Bronx County Historical Society Research Library*

ALLERTON AVENUE BETWEEN THROOP AND BOUCK AVENUES has a suburban air in July, 1963. Single family homes with neatly trimmed hedges are found in a neighborhood of trees, little automobile traffic, and no traffic lights at intersections. The elevated structure at the base of the hill is the Dyre Avenue line of the New York City subway system.   *The Bronx County Historical Society Research Library*

172ND STREET AT THE INTERSECTION OF INWOOD AND CROMWELL AVENUES
in the Highbridge neighborhood in the early 1950s is dominated by a six-story
Art Deco style apartment house. More Art Deco buildings can be seen further
down Inwood Avenue to the left, while garages and service stations occupy much
of Cromwell Avenue to the right. The roofs of all the residences are studded
with television antennas. Cars are parked almost everywhere along the curbside.
One woman in the sidewalk to the left, who has completed her shopping, is
carrying her purchases in a shopping bag, while a man is crossing at the
intersection to the right with a baby's stroller filled with cartons.

HOLLAND AVENUE NORTH OF NORTH OAK DRIVE in April, 1964 is flanked by two-story frame houses. Yet, a few blocks to the north rise the Gun Hill Houses piercing the horizon to the left. The twin towers of the Immaculate Conception Roman Catholic Church on Gun Hill Road dominates the vista on the other side of the street.

ON THE WEST SIDE OF MORRIS AVENUE, BETWEEN 152ND AND 153RD STREETS, stands a series of three-to five-story apartment houses, most with street level shops in the mid-1960s. These include a barber shop, with its striped pole on the sidewalk, a store selling slip covers, another selling ices, and a luncheonette on the corner of 153rd Street. A truck delivers Ballantine Ale to the right, while the cars at the curb park next to parking meters.

143RD STREET AND MORRIS AVENUE is the site of the Lester Patterson Houses in January, 1952. On either corner are two of the many expanses of lawns and trees, some with park benches, to delight the eye and serve as recreation for the tenants of this low income housing project. Parked cars take every available space at the curbside of 143rd Street. The vista ends at Third Avenue, where residents may cross the street to shop at the Jefferson Food Center.

AT THE CORNER OF CONCOURSE VILLAGE WEST AND 156TH STREET in the mid-1960s, local citizens watch as a new stop sign is cemented into place. In the rear rises the Concourse Village cooperative apartment complex, with the terraces on each floor clearly visible.

The Bronx County Historical Society Research Library

161ST STREET BETWEEN SHERIDAN AND SHERMAN AVENUES is the location
of the Plaza Service Center in the mid-1960s. Selling Mobil gasoline at
34 cents a gallon and giving Plaid Stamps as premiums for purchases, it not
only serves local residents, but also the heavy traffic on 161st Street.
Across the street is the excavated site of the New York Central Railroad yards.
The structure to the left whose roof extends above the street level and
sports a tall brick chimney was built to service the trains. Further down the
yards is a platform upon which the tall Concourse Village cooperative
apartments stand. One of the amenities offered buyers is a terrace.
The apartment complex to the left is the Melrose Houses project.

The Bronx County Historical Society
Research Library

PARKCHESTER ALONG MCCRAW AVENUE is in varying stages of construction in May, 1939. The buildings in the foreground have just recently had their steel skeletons erected, while those in the background are already being clad in red brick.

PARKCHESTER'S NEW APARTMENTS ON METROPOLITAN OVAL
receive a shipment of new stoves in September, 1940. Work is still
continuing to complete the massive housing complex.

THE BATHROOMS IN PARKCHESTER have all the latest designs when the model apartment is opened for inspection in December, 1938. Most notable is the bathtub gleaming in the light coming through the widow above it. The showerhead emerges from the righthand wall from pipes located inside the structure. The tiled floor consists of two colors arranged in a pattern of squares.

KITCHENS IN THE NEW PARKCHESTER HOUSING development in 1938 are all white and equipped with the latest appliances. A gas range is to the right, a double sink in the center, and a refrigerator to the left. The window over the counter allows sunshine in, while the cabinets over the sink are ready for use to hold dishes, pots and food.

METROPOLITAN AVENUE IN PARKCHESTER'S SOUTH QUADRANT is the home of the new Loew's American movie theater in January, 1941. The marquee advertises a double feature with Gary Cooper and Madelene Carroll in "Northwest Mounted Police" and Paulette Goddard and Dick Powell in "Christmas in July." The theater building, bearing bas reliefs on its facade and clad in gleaming tile, is part of a shopping district in the massive housing complex, whose red brick buildings rise above it. Shops line the streets, including the Parkchester News Company store to the right, which sells cigars, stationery, and greeting cards, as well as newspapers, and sports a lending library. There is little traffic in the street except for a delivery truck with its rear doors open to the left. Cars are parked head-in toward the curb.

The Bronx County Historical Society
Research Library

The Bronx County Historical Society
Research Library

METROPOLITAN OVAL IN PARKCHESTER is the focus of recreation
in May, 1942. Residents of the massive housing complex, just recently
completed, enjoy the pool in the center of the oval, with its fountain
featuring spouting fish producing a pleasant splashing sound.
While some people walk around the oval, admiring the blooming
flowers on the far side of the pool, others sit on the benches facing the
water and engage in conversation with family and neighbors.

WORKMEN PLACE A STREET SIGN to a lamppost on February 29, 1940 designating the street below as Metropolitan Avenue, which is named in honor of The Metropolitan Life Insurance Company, the company that built Parkchester. One of the new buildings with casement windows and terra cotta window frames is in the background. When completed Parkchester was the largest housing development in the country.

The Bronx County Historical Society
Research Library
—Arthur Seifert, photographer

LOCUST POINT ON THROGGS NECK is filled with long bungalow-type houses in 1946. Several of those closest to Long Island Sound have piers available to moor boats. A few residents use the empty spaces between homes as gardens to plant vegetables. Only three cars can be seen parked along Tierney Place, the first roadway paralleling the waterfront, while none can be observed along Giegerich Place, one block away.

ON SHERIDAN AVENUE AND 162ND STREET rise a number of Art Deco apartment houses, built in the 1930s, and still considered highly desirable residences in the late 1950s. By that time, however, every bit of curb space is filled with parked cars, leaving little room for one moving automobile to pass another when cars are double parked.

The Bronx County Historical
Society Research Library
−Arthur Seifert, photographer

JUST OFF BRUCKNER BOULEVARD IN CLASON POINT is a whole
community of quonset huts erected by the New York City Housing
Authority to accommodate veterans returning from World War II
and their families. Each hut could accommodate two separate families.

MORRIS PLACE AT PARK AVENUE, a small street between 169th and 170th Streets, was the site of some nineteenth century frame houses in February, 1956. Its eastern end is blocked off from Washington Avenue by the rear of a structure used as a social hall. Despite its size, one curb of the narrow street is completely flanked by parked cars. Nevertheless, the area is scheduled for a major change, since the man standing in the middle of the roadway holding a sign with the legend "P132" is aiding a surveyor for the New York City Housing Authority. The street is scheduled to be removed and replaced by the Gouverneur Morris housing project.

The Bronx County Historical Society Research Library

AT 146TH STREET AT THE INTERSECTION OF WALTON AVENUE stands a charming old mansion that is for sale in 1939. The property is graced by a spacious lawn with trees and a wooden fence. Behind it, however, in this heavily industrialized Mott Haven section is an automobile wrecker and a freight station.

The Bronx County Historical Society Research Library

THE GRAND CONCOURSE NEAR 164TH STREET in the early 1960s is
flanked by many Art Deco style apartment houses, as can be seen to
the lower right. In the center left is the broad expanse of Joyce Kilmer
Park. Beyond that, across 161st Street, stands the Bronx County
Building. Beyond the apartment houses to the right and center is
Yankee Stadium. To the right of the stadium, and behind the apartment
buildings, can be seen the baseball diamond of Babe Ruth Stadium.
Beyond it can be seen the end of Jerome Avenue rising to become
the approach road to the Macombs Dam Bridge going over the
Harlem River to Manhattan.

Schools

HUNTER COLLEGE IN THE BRONX at the western end of Bedford Park Boulevard acts as the headquarters of the United Nations in 1946. Cars of diplomats and international civil servants are parked in the traffic circle, whose focal point is the flagpole to the right. To the right of the flagpole, part of Student Hall can be seen, while Gillet Hall rises toward the center of the photograph. The Jerome Park Reservoir lies beyond it to the left. On the other side are the one- and two-family homes and scattered apartment houses of the Kingsbridge Heights neighborhood.

The Bronx County Historical Society Research Library

THE GLEE CLUB OF P.S. 21 ON 225TH STREET NEAR WHITE PLAINS ROAD, performs in the school's auditorium in the early 1950s. Some pupils from the surrounding Williamsbridge neighborhood at the left watch the teacher, Mrs. M. Louise Heffernan, in front of the piano lead the choir through its song.

PUPILS IN P.S. 8 on Briggs Avenue near Mosholu Parkway on February 8, 1949 move the walls of their classrooms on slide tracks on the floor and ceiling to create a larger assembly-room space. A piano sits on a raised platform to the left. Inside the classroom, the pupils, with girls placed on one side and boys on the other, sit at the desks which are bolted to the floor and arranged in rows.

The Bronx County Historical Society Research Library

AT PUTNAM AVENUE BETWEEN 238TH AND 240TH STREETS in front of Visitation Roman Catholic Church and School in Kingsbridge stand girls who will participate in their First Communion in 1942. The attached houses to the left face Bailey Avenue.

The Bronx County Historical Society Research Library
—Gobba Beirne Collection

P.S. 14 ON **HOLLYWOOD AVENUE** IN **THROGGS NECK** in 1946 faces empty lots of razed houses in preparation for the widening of Bruckner Boulevard. Consequently, the school and its concrete yard, in which a few children are playing, are almost surrounded by empty lots. There is little traffic on Hollywood Avenue, and none at all on Crosby Avenue behind the school.

The Bronx County Historical Society
Research Library
—Arthur Seifert, photographer

AT 244TH STREET in the exclusive and affluent neighborhood of
Fieldston stands the Barnard School for Boys in the mid-1930s.
Set amid manicured lawns and shady trees, the mansion-like school
building provides a pleasant place for the boys to learn. To the left,
above the stone retaining wall, is the play area surrounded by a
fence. The school's bus is parked beyond.

The Bronx County Historical Society
Research Library
—Arthur Seifert, photographer

P.S. 119 STANDS AT PUGSLEY AND BLACKROCK AVENUES in Unionport surrounded by empty lots in 1946. Beside the wide open spaces and streets empty of all traffic and parked cars, the area is dominated by one- and two-family homes and some small apartment houses.

ON FORDHAM ROAD in the heart of the commercial business district is the Drake Business School in 1956. Here, in its classrooms above the busy shops, Bronx Borough President Joseph F. Periconi tries out a new IBM electric typewriter while Frank March, the school's owner and publisher of *Life in the Bronx* magazine, hovers over him and Dr. David Steinman looks on from behind.

The Bronx County Historical Society
Research Library
—Max Levine Collection

ON SEDGWICK AVENUE SOUTH OF PEROT STREET in Kingsbridge Heights stands Junior High School 143. Here, in the early 1960s, the music class stands on the auditorium stage after a concert receiving the plaudits of the proud parents in the audience.

MOSHOLU AVENUE AND 255TH STREET is the site of a playground located
behind P.S. 81 to the left and Riverdale Neighborhood House to the
right about 1950. While the field in the foreground and to the right has
just had its grass mowed, youngsters cavort in the playground in the center.
Several boys occupy the area near the rear of the school, which is laid out
in basketball and shuffleboard courts. Beyond the fence to the right is
the Riverdale Neighborhood House pool and tennis courts.

JAMES MONROE HIGH SCHOOL dominates Boynton Avenue in the
Soundview neighborhood in 1946. The school's athletic field is to its rear,
flanking Manor Avenue. To the left, is P.S. 77. The rest of the area is
filled with semi-detached homes and apartment houses.

The Bronx County Historical Society
Research Library
–Arthur Seifert, photographer

KEATING HALL ON THE FORDHAM UNIVERSITY CAMPUS overlooks the large field upon which students dressed in their ROTC uniforms are standing in formation on a day in the 1950s. A crowd is massed on the steps of the building to watch the proceedings.

An Elementary School Class in P.S. 21 at East 225th Street in the 1950s is studying a diorama and noting in their books what they observe. The standing boy on the extreme right intently studying a book is wearing a belt over his shoulder upon which is affixed a metal school-crossing-guard badge.

*The Bronx County Historical Society
Research Library*

THE COLLEGE OF MOUNT SAINT VINCENT along the Hudson River in Riverdale remains a higher education facility for women operated by the Sisters of Charity, in 1940. The ivy-covered Fonthill Castle to the right serves as the library, while most of the classes are held in the large brick structure behind it, marked by the spired tower in the center. The gazebo to the left is topped by a cross and shelters a statue. The hilly grounds are beautifully landscaped with a variety of trees and plants.

BRUCKNER BOULEVARD AT THE CORNER OF HOLLYWOOD AND LAYTON AVENUES shows increasing automobile traffic in 1956, but with enough safety to allow a boy riding his bicycle to the left. Near him, billboards advertise Shell gasoline and Rheingold beer. On the opposite corner, in the center, a new light pole with a curving arm has been erected, which contrasts with the more ornate straight-arm poles installed decades earlier. P.S. 14 is the four-story building dominating the street, while the spire of the Lutheran Church on Baisley Avenue punctuates the skyline in the center.

BRONX BOROUGH PRESIDENT JAMES J. LYONS speaks at the platform during the opening ceremonies of the new Albert Einstein College of Medicine of Yeshiva University off Eastchester Road on October 25, 1955.

A TWO-STORY TAXPAYER occupies the north side of East Fordham Road between Morris and Creston Avenues in the 1950s. The Naegeli Shops are holding a sale on furniture. Also on that block are the Bostonian Shoe Shop and The Corset Shop farther down the street. On the floor above are Arthur Murray's Dance Studio, whose slogan was, "Arthur Murray taught me dancing in a hurry," and the Mister Caterer.

The Bronx County Historical Society
Research Library
—Max Levine Collection

An Ethnic Feast

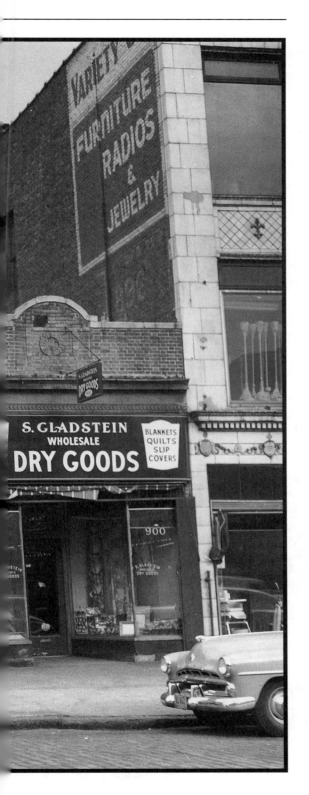

PROSPECT AVENUE NEAR 162ND STREET is a local shopping area around 1950. To the left, can be seen part of the Hollywood Clothes store, specializing in men's suits displayed in the store window. To its right is the Chinese-American Restaurant, which advertises chop suey and chow mein. To its right is Frank's Ladies and Mens clothing store. One window shows mens' suits, while the other features ladies' dresses and coats. Next to it is S. Gladstein's wholesale dry goods store, featuring draperies, curtains, bedspreads, linens, blankets, quilts, and slip covers.

The Bronx County Historical Society Research Library

ON THE GRAND CONCOURSE BETWEEN 188TH STREET AND FORDHAM ROAD
is Krum's, famous for its candies and ice cream sodas. One section of the store is a
sales area flanked with display cases filled with Krum's chocolate confections
made in its own kitchens. Beyond, down a small set of stairs, is the section where
people could order delicious ice cream sodas and sundaes and eat them at the counter.
For decades, teenagers on a date would stop at Krum's after seeing a motion
picture double feature at the Paradise Theater across the street.

ON 152ND STREET BETWEEN MELROSE AND THIRD AVENUES in the Hub section in the mid-1960s stands a series
of frame apartment houses with false brick or shingle fronts. While the busy stores on nearby Third Avenue cater to
people from all over The Bronx, the shops at the street level of these buildings serve the residents. The one in the
center advertises pizza, coffee, Coca Cola, and Ballantine and Rheingold beers. *The Bronx County Historical Society Research Library*

ON BOSTON ROAD NEAR PELHAM PARKWAY stands the Post Road Casino with its canopied entrance in the mid-1930s. Parking is available for some customers in the lot to the right. Patrons are offered beer and liquor at the bar, and dining and dancing in the restaurant. The specialty of the house is its genuine Italian spaghetti.

FTELY AVENUE AND THE CORNER OF BRUCKNER BOULEVARD is the scene of the construction of the Bruckner Expressway about 1956. Both large trucks and passenger cars move along the new roadway. Across the street is a White Castle, home of the twelve cent hamburger, which also advertises that it serves hot coffee for ten cents. The housing development in the center and to the right is the Bronxdale Houses.

*The Bronx County Historical Society
Research Library*

THE PELL TREE INN ALONG SHORE ROAD IN PELHAM BAY PARK is a popular road house and restaurant in the 1930s. While patrons dined seated on bentwood chairs at tablecloth covered tables, a piano player or a small band would play popular favorites.

AT BOSTON ROAD AND BRONXWOOD AVENUE about 1950 stands the Glass Post Bar and Restaurant, which shares its structure with a neighboring liquor store and an A&P Supermarket. Across the street to the left is a White Castle, which specializes in serving inexpensive hamburgers. There is little automobile traffic in this largely residential neighborhood in the eastern part of The Bronx. Brick apartment residences rise over these local shops, and their roofs are studded with metal antennas each tenant had to erect to obtain clear reception for a television set. Electricity to the neighborhood is supplied by overhead wires strung along wooden poles erected along the sidewalk.

The Bronx County Historical Society Research Library

AT THE CORNER OF PROSPECT AVENUE AND 151ST STREET about 1950,
a Spanish American Restaurant serves the local Puerto Rican populace.
A sign placed in the window advertises the appearance of three Latin bands
at the Tropicana Club.

The Bronx County Historical Society
Research Library

ON LAYTON AVENUE AT THE NORTHERN CORNER OF EASTERN BOULEVARD (later, Bruckner Boulevard) stands Mumm's Candy Store, a local gathering spot for neighborhood children. Mr. Mumm, the proprietor, stands on the left, while Mr. Schmidt is on the right. Just coming from school the two boys, wearing ties and jackets, and the girl in her sweater and skirt, have stopped in for a treat in the 1930s. An ice cream soda cost ten cents, while customers had to pay five cents more for a plain frappe, a plate of ice cream, a Neapolitan brick, or a marshmallow frappe.

WESTCHESTER AVENUE NEAR ROGERS PLACE AND 163RD STREET is the location of the Tropicana Club in 1951. It features food, entertainment and dancing for the growing Puerto Rican population in the surrounding neighborhood. A sign printed in Spanish posted to the left of the name of the club in the center informs patrons that "The Hispanic Voice of the Air" program broadcasts every Sunday from there over radio station WWRL. Below it, similar Spanish language signs advertise the acts performing at the club every Friday, Saturday, and Sunday. The canopied entrance to the establishment is at the left. A Rheingold Beer truck is delivering its cargo to the center right, mostly obscured by the truck in the roadway.

At the time, the old trolley tracks are being ripped up from the roadbed of Westchester Avenue. The steel superstructure above, which casts its shadow on the Tropicana Club, is the White Plains Road elevated line of the Lexington and Seventh Avenue subways.

AT THE INTERSECTION OF 186TH STREET AND CRESCENT AND BELMONT AVENUES in the Belmont neighborhood in 1957 there are street level shops to service tenants living in surrounding apartment houses. Cars are parked along the curbs of Crescent Avenue in front and Belmont Avenue straight ahead. A grocery store occupies the apex of the triangle of Crescent Avenue and 186th Street to the left, while across the street, there is a candy store. A meat market occupies the apex of Crescent and Belmont Avenues to the right. The trees at the end of the vista of Belmont Avenue mark the Fordham University campus, while the tower topped with a square cupola one block up Belmont Avenue to the left is the corner of Mount Carmel Roman Catholic Church.   *The Bronx County Historical Society Research Library*

*The Bronx County Historical Society
Research Library*

BAILEY AVENUE AND KINGSBRIDGE ROAD in December, 1952, is the site of the construction of P.S. 122 across Kingsbridge Road. A bus is on its way to Broadway and the City Line as it passes in front of the new structure, while a passenger car is making a turn onto Bailey Avenue. The Kingsbridge Tavern occupies the corner to the left, while a mail box is affixed to the lightpole to the right.

HOWARD JOHNSON'S RESTAURANT occupies the corner of Southern Boulevard at Fordham Road across the street from an entrance to the Bronx Zoo in the 1950s. Fordham Hospital is on the right in the background. The Southern Boulevard trolley tracks have been partially covered with asphalt, in the foreground. *The Bronx County Historical Society Research Library*

The Bronx County Historical Society Research Library

AT THE DOG-EE-DEN DRIVE-IN-RESTAURANT ON BRUCKNER BOULEVARD around 1956, the price of sandwiches is 70 cents for a meatball hero to $1.00 for a veal cutlet parmagana, with lettuce and tomato 10 cents extra, and a soda for 15 or 25 cents.

Civic
Life

The Bronx County Historical Society
Research Library

CASTLE HILL AVENUE NEAR WESTCHESTER AVENUE is the scene of a Little League parade on an early spring day in the 1950s. Behind the color guard is a band from Edgewater Park on Throggs Neck followed by each team in the league in formation. The presence of people in the roadway does little to disrupt the flow of traffic on the wide thoroughfare. There is enough parking at the curbside for motorists who wish to pull aside to watch, while some pedestrians halt their shopping to observe the scene. The street is flanked by local shops, such as a Singer sewing machine store, a Fisher-Beer five and ten cent store, and an upholsterer.

The five-story apartment house in the center sports an outdoor sign advertising Ruppert's Knickerbocker Beer. To the right, the Castle Hill theater is showing a motion picture double feature. On the horizon to the right rise the twin domes of St. Raymond's Roman Catholic Church at the corner of Tremont Avenue.

The tall apartment house on the horizon to the left is part of Parkchester.

*The Bronx County Historical Society
Research Library
—Max Levine Collection*

ON THE GRAND CONCOURSE IN FRONT OF THE POE GARAGE, Dwight D. Eisenhower campaigns for President in the fall of 1952. To the left is his host, former State Senator and Bronx Republican County Chairman Paul A. Fino.

AT THE CONCOURSE PLAZA HOTEL Francis Cardinal Spellman and New York City Mayor Robert Wagner greet Bronx Borough President Joseph F. Periconi at the dais during a reception in 1964 celebrating the Golden Jubilee of Bronx County. The special Golden Jubilee banner is affixed to the wall above the heads of the dignitaries. *The Bronx County Historical Society Research Library*

ON THE GRAND CONCOURSE NEAR 188TH STREET, in front of Krum's, the maker of chocolates and the seller of ice cream, Congressman Isadore Dollinger and Bronx Borough President James J. Lyons examine the latest issue of *Life in The Bronx,* the only magazine produced in the borough about Bronxites. Featured on the cover are photographs of prominent members of the New York Yankees who helped the team win its record-breaking fifth World Series in a row in 1953.

ON MILES AVENUE NEAR MEAGHER AVENUE on Throggs Neck in the 1950s stands the hall of the Theodore Korony Post of the American Legion. Cars fill half the parking lot in front of the one-story structure to attend an event. The American flag flies proudly from the flagpole in the middle of the lot. Except for a few single and two-family homes, the area appears almost uninhabited, with trees and electrical wires dominating the landscape. *The Bronx County Historical Society Research Library*

THE CONCOURSE PLAZA HOTEL was the site of many major events in the late 1950s and early 1960s. Here, inside the hotel, at the Urban League of Greater New York's eighth annual luncheon, awards are presented for their efforts to achieve cooperation between people of all races, creeds, and colors to Bronx businessman Elias Karmon to the left and Bronx realtor J. Clarence Davies, Jr., to the right.
In the center are Walter H. Gladwin, who served as a State Assemblyman from The Bronx from 1954 to 1957, and former First Lady, Eleanor Roosevelt.

AT THE BRONX COUNTY REPUBLICAN PARTY DINNER in 1965, all of the prominent Republicans gather. Standing in the front are, from left to right, New York City Councilman-at-Large A. Joseph Ribustello, Bronx Borough President Joseph F. Periconi, Congressman and Bronx County Republican Party Chairman Paul A. Fino, New York State Governor Nelson A. Rockefeller, and New York State Senate candidate John D. Calandra.

KINGSBRIDGE ROAD JUST WEST OF JEROME AVENUE is the site of the massive Kingsbridge Armory, seen across the street, in December, 1952. Parked cars crowd all available space along the curb of both sides of the street. Above the cars and behind the armory in the center is the Fordham Manor Dutch Reformed Church. To its left, and partially obscured by the streetlamp, is a six-story apartment house in the Art Deco style. *The Bronx County Historical Society Research Library*

125

NEAR THE END OF MANIDA STREET BETWEEN RYAWA AVENUE AND
THE EAST RIVER people gather on November 5, 1951 for the dedication
ceremonies of the Hunts Point Sewage Treatment Plant. A uniformed
band serenades the people in the audience seated on wooden folding
chairs and the dignitaries on the temporary covered platform decorated
with red, white, and blue bunting. The new plant rises to the right.
In the background to the left are some of the factories found in
this section of the Hunts Point peninsula.

The Bronx County Historical Society
Research Library

THE BRONX COUNTY DEMOCRATIC DINNERS in the mid-1950s always brought out prominent elected and appointed public officials and businessmen. These were the men who made the most important decisions affecting The Bronx, an overwhelmingly Democratic-voting area. Seated here, left to right, are New York State Comptroller Arthur Levitt, Governor Averell Harriman, Mayor Robert Wagner, and Congressman and Bronx Democratic Chairman Charles Buckley. Standing behind them, left to right, are Cornelius J. Walsh and Charles J. Bensley, both Bronx members of the New York City Board of Education, Bronx Borough President James J. Lyons, New York Secretary of State Carmine DeSapio, New York State Lieutenant Governor George B. DeLuca, who was from The Bronx, Max J. Schneider, Bronx District Attorney Daniel Sullivan, Thomas Lynch, who was Vice President of the Chase Manhattan Bank, and New York City Comptroller, Lawrence E. Gerosa, who was also a Bronxite.

THE CONCOURSE PLAZA HOTEL on the wide Grand Concourse at 161st Street is the social center of The Bronx in 1939. Its cafe and bar on the corner is a favorite meeting place for lawyers and public officials working in the nearby Bronx County Building. The sign on the traffic island announces that the Bronx Kiwanis Club met in the hotel. Two women are crossing the street toward the benches of Joyce Kilmer Park.

HERMAN BADILLO, the first Puerto Rican elected President of the Borough of The Bronx in 1965, is greeted by Congressman Jacob Gilbert.

The Bronx County Historical Society
Research Library
—Max Levine Collection

BATHGATE AVENUE NEAR 178TH STREET is filled with people following a Victory Parade in the summer of 1942. A small platform is set up on the sidewalk at the recess of the apartment house. Some of the residents observe the proceedings from fire escapes and windows. Five youngsters have climbed the wooden steps of a frame house across the street. Other neighborhood inhabitants mill about prior to the start of the program. The street is decorated with two large flags, some pennants, and a specially designed banner.

The Bronx County Historical Society
Research Library
—Baxter Collection

The Bronx County Historical Society
Research Library
–Max Levine Collection

THE BRONX LIONS CLUB holds a midday rally promoting the purchase of defense bonds at the Fordham Road overpass of the Grand Concourse in the 1950s. Across the street is the U.S. Army recruiting station. At the southeast corner of the intersection is the Wagner Building, which houses the Drake Secretarial School and, on the street level, a variety of shops, including a cafeteria, a cigar and paper store, and a florist.

WILLIAMSBRIDGE ROAD AT WARING AVENUE is blocked by a wall of mothers, some with their children in a stroller or a carriage, demanding that the stop sign on the corner by replaced by a traffic light in the 1950s. Most of them live in the Pelham Parkway Houses, and their signs request motorists to detour so their children can be safe. *The Bronx County Historical Society Research Library*

THE COMMERCIAL BUILDING AT 189TH STREET AND PARK AVENUE is the home of The North End Democratic Club in 1960. The club, on the second floor, displays a large poster with the names of the candidates of the 1960 elections prominently displayed. On the street level is the U.S. Post Office Fordham Station. *The Bronx County Historical Society Research Library*

HUGE CROWDS GATHER on the Grand Concourse south of Fordham Road in front of the Wagner Building to hear presidential candidate John F. Kennedy speak in 1960. The center roadway leading under the Concourse beneath Fordham Road remains clear of traffic. The plush Loew's Paradise Theater is to the center left.

The Bronx County Historical Society
Research Library
—Max Levine Collection

JOHN F. KENNEDY shakes the hand of a local policeman as he stops at the Grand Concourse and 162nd Street during his campaign for president in 1960. Seated in the car is New York City Mayor Robert F. Wagner, Jr.

The Bronx County Historical Society
Research Library

Recreation

AT 166TH STREET BETWEEN OGDEN AND UNIVERSITY AVENUES in Highbridge officials, coaches, and some players in the Highbridge Little League gather on Labor Day 1957 to mark the games that will be played there to determine the league's champion. Signs on the fence prominently display the names of the local merchants who sponsor the Little League. The largest sign, occupying the place of honor in this predominantly Irish neighborhood, is Division 9 of the Ancient Order of Hibernians, whose name is symbolically enclosed in a huge green shamrock. The apartment houses that fill much of the neighborhood can be seen beyond the fence.

*The Bronx County Historical Society
Research Library*

EDENWALD in the northeast Bronx still sported a rural atmosphere
in the winter of 1937. Here, Joe Sauter, who lived in Melrose in the
southwestern part of The Bronx, can take two children out in a
horse-drawn sleigh for a ride.

THE BRONX ZOO regularly attracts
millions of visitors over the years.
One of the popular attractions are the
Indian elephants, and, one summer in
the 1940s, a young elephant was so
eager to obtain peanuts offered by
spectators that it partially climbed
on top of the wall of the outdoor
pen to be able to reach the preferred
goodies. The pen is in front of
the ornate Elephant House.

*The Bronx County Historical Society
Research Library
–Cyrus Getter Association Collection*

IN THE BRONX ZOO, a ride on a two humped camel, led by a uniform attendant is one of the main attractions for children in the 1950s. The beautifully sculpted Elephant House is in the background.

The Bronx County Historical Society
Research Library

BRONX PARK EAST NEAR 233RD STREET on June 25, 1950 is the site of a playground where neighborhood children could enjoy swings, seesaws, a jungle gym, and a slide for their amusement, as well as a water fountain. Parents tending baby carriages sit on the benches watching the older children play. Woodlawn Cemetery is in the background.

INDIAN LAKE IN CROTONA PARK is a pleasant place to relax in a summer in the mid-1930s. One man is reading a book while sitting on a bench by the side of the lake, while another sits on a bench beneath the trees to the right. The house up a few stone steps from the lakeside has public telephones. To the right is a pier with rowboats moored there that can be rented for rowing on the lake. The road to the left traverses the park along Prospect Avenue between the lake and the athletic field.

The Bronx County Historical Society
Research Library

THE HILLS OF THE GOLF COURSE IN VAN CORTLANDT PARK
are turned into ski slopes and a ski school in the winter of 1963.
At the top of the hill rises the Amalgamated Houses, a cooperative
development along Van Cortlandt Park South.

MORRIS PARK AVENUE BETWEEN HAIGHT AND TOMLINSON AVENUES in the early 1950s is the site of the Alfred Loreto Playground. The section nearest Morris Park Avenue to the left is laid out in a baseball field and basketball courts, one of which is being used. The section separated from it by a fence to the right is filled with children using playground equipment. The area is surrounded by one- and two-family homes. The ones along Morris Park Avenue to the right have their living quarters located above street level shops, including a delicatessen and a shoe repair shop.   *The Bronx County Historical Society Research Library*

The Bronx County Historical Society Research Library
—New York City Parks Department

AT ORCHARD BEACH, the bathouses and ball fields and water attracts thousands of Bronxites daily after it opened in Pelham Bay Park in 1937. The monumental columned entrance leads to a plaza with facilities for picnicking near a central flagpole. The approach to the entrance is an oval driveway flanked with newly-planted trees.

CROWDS FILL YANKEE STADIUM for a spring day's game at 161st Street and River Avenue in the 1950s, while automobiles fill the parking lots along the streets and the garages near the famed ball park. The baseball diamonds outside the stadium are in Macombs Dam Park.

YANKEE STADIUM during the first game of the 1947 World Series has every seat filled, even in the bleachers. Beyond the advertising billboards to the left center is the 161st Street elevated station of the Woodlawn-Jerome line of the Lexington Avenue subway. People are lined up at the edge of the platform overlooking the bleachers and the field to see the game from "the world's largest knothole." The game is in the fourth inning. The visiting Brooklyn Dodgers have just completed their half of the inning, and the New York Yankees are coming to bat. At the base of the flagpole on the field to the left are two monuments, one to former manager Miller Huggins, and the other to former first baseman Lou Gehrig. The scoreboard towering over the bleacher seats to the right is operated manually, with men in the space behind the display slipping printed numbers in and out of slots as the game progresses. Among the advertisements on the billboards is one for the Bronx Savings Bank at Tremont and Park Avenues.

Courtesy of the New York Yankees
–Bob Olen

The Bronx County Historical Society
Research Library

THE PLAYGROUND OF THE SEDGWICK HOUSES ON UNIVERSITY AVENUE NEAR THE WASHINGTON BRIDGE in the early 1950s has equipment for the enjoyment of all ages, including handball and basketball courts, monkey bars and other climbing apparatus, see saws and a slide-upon. Traffic is beginning to congest the area where the bridge approach and several Bronx streets converge. To the center right is traffic on the approach to the bridge leading to and from 181st Street in Manhattan. Perpendicular to the approach to the left is University Avenue. Angling off from it is Ogden Avenue and, to the extreme left, Edward L. Grant Highway. Between the last two is a branch of the Bank of the Manhattan Company. In front of that is a traffic island bearing a flagpole and a statue of a World War I soldier erected as a monument to those from the Highbridge neighborhood who died in that conflict. Beyond rise the many five- and six-story apartment houses that fill Highbridge. The structure that gave the neighborhood its name, the High Bridge, can be seen in the upper right hand corner as it crosses the Harlem River.

ON EAST 177TH STREET AND LONGSTREET AVENUE in Throggs Neck stands the building housing the Bronx Beach and Pool in 1965. For decades, it was a mecca for people from the area and surrounding neighborhoods.

The Bronx County Historical Society Research Library–Schleissman Collection

FREEDOMLAND in the northeast Bronx is under construction in April, 1960. Here, in the midst of what was a swamp, rise the nineteenth century facades of the "Little Old New York" street that will welcome visitors to this amusement park designed to be Disneyland of the east coast.

FREEDOMLAND, the world's largest amusement park, dominated the
northeast corner of The Bronx on the west bank of the Hutchinson River in
July, 1962. Shaped like the map of the United States, the park attempted
to make its visitors experience the history of the country in its attractions.
The entrance led patrons to "Little Old New York," whose buildings'
facades attempted to recreate the look of the metropolis in the late
nineteenth century. There, amusement-seekers could take a horsecar
for ten cents to a facsimile of the Great Chicago Fire in the center
of the park.

The Bronx County Historical Society
Research Library
—Bassein Collection

WILLIAMSBRIDGE OVAL PARK is only recently-opened in September, 1937. Converted from a reservoir, a chain link fence cordons off the athletic field and track in the center of the Oval. The park also features playgrounds, tennis, horseshoe courts and picnic areas. Playgrounds where children are playing are to the left and right. The large structure at the edge near the center houses meeting rooms, lockers and rest rooms. Outside the park, on Van Cortlandt Avenue East and Mosholu Parkway, stands P.S. 80. Apartment houses in this Norwood neighborhood otherwise dominate the scene.

SOUTHERN BOULEVARD AND FORDHAM ROAD is the site of a neighborhood carnival in the 1950s. Many of the children enjoying themselves probably attend P.S. 74 in the background to the left. While friendly policemen and parents look on, children pay ten cents apiece to ride in a boat on a small artificial pond, ride a merry-go-round, or any of the other carnival rides.

The Bronx County Historical Society
Research Library
—Max Levine Collection

THE CASTLE HILL DAY CAMP AT THE FOOT OF SOUNDVIEW AVENUE provides many Bronx children with summers of fun starting in the 1940s. Here, in a publicity photograph, a girl camper, wearing the insignia of the camp, an Indian chief's head in full feathered headdress, and carrying her lunchbox, holds the hands of her counselor, while her beaming mother looks on.

The Bronx County Historical Society Research Library

CAMPERS AT THE CASTLE HILL DAY CAMP, located on the East River at the foot of Castle Hill Avenue, enjoy a dip in a pool in the 1950s.

The Bronx County Historical Society Research Library

CASTLE HILL BEACH CLUB AT THE FOOT OF CASTLE HILL AVENUE was known as the Castle Hill Bathing Park in 1941. Here, the season's champion swimmers in the fifty-yard event pose for the camera. From left to right, at the top is Rhoda Brand, Leah Levine, Pearl Landau, William Jordan, Joseph Kiesel, and Martin Steinberg. At the bottom is Tony Nicolini, Wesley Bray and Herbert Shedlin.

The Bronx County Historical Society Research Library

SHOREHAVEN BEACH CLUB AT THE FOOT OF SOUNDVIEW AVENUE was a popular private resort in the 1950s and 1960s. It boasted of a large salt water pool and many athletic facilities. However, a major attraction came late in the season with the Miss Shorehaven contest. Here, standing on the stage where two outdoor musical performances were offered every afternoon, is Miss Shorehaven of 1958 with the two runners-up.

The Bronx County Historical Society Research Library
−Randy Ross, photographer

THE PLAYGROUND AT 254TH STREET AND MOSHOLU AVENUE in Riverdale is a pleasant spot for parents to take their children about 1950. Parents can sit around a long bench as they watch youngsters play in a sandbox guarded by an iron fence. For the amusement of the children, there are also two slide-upons, a set of monkey bars, and several swings. A flagpole and restrooms round out the facilities available. The entire playground, near P.S. 81, is bordered by a grove of beautiful trees.

The Bronx County Historical Society
Research Library

THE INDOOR RECREATION CENTER IN ST. MARY'S PARK is a magnet for the children of the neighborhood in the early 1950s. As the afternoon sun floods the space through the high windows facing St. Anns Avenue, some of them participate in ping pong games, while others watch and socialize.

*The Bronx County Historical Society
Research Library*

The Bronx County Historical Society
Research Library
—Max Levine Collection

Entertainment and Culture

TREMONT AVENUE BETWEEN DAVIDSON AND JEROME AVENUES is a local shopping street undergoing change in 1964. At the corner of Davidson Avenue, the Art Delicatessen and Grocery bears a sign that it will be opening soon. Further to the right, past Dave's Pants and Outerware store, the University Sign store, a storefront doctor's office, and the luncheonette, is an empty shop with a sign in the window advertising that the space is for rent. At the rounded corner of Jerome Avenue stands the air conditioned Art Theater with its marquee announcing its current double feature, Henry Fonda and Cliff Robertson in "The Best Man," and "Man's Favorite Sport." The elevated structure to the right is the Woodlawn-Jerome line of the Lexington Avenue subway. Traffic is not only filling Tremont Avenue, a major thoroughfare, but practically clogs Davidson Avenue to the left, especially with cars parked at every available spot along the curb.

THE EDGAR ALLAN POE COTTAGE in Poe Park was the last home
of the famous poet, short story writer, and inventor of the detective story.
In the summer of 1944, thousands of Bronx residents and tourists would
make the pilgrimage to the modest frame home to see how the writer lived.
Behind the cottage rise the apartment houses at the corner of the
Grand Concourse and Kingsbridge Road.

The Bronx County Historical Society
Research Library

THIS PARKING AREA IS AT THE POINT WHERE RESERVOIR OVAL EAST
MEETS RESERVOIR OVAL WEST parallel to Bainbridge Avenue in 1963.
Behind the iron fence rises the grassy wall of the Williamsbridge Oval Park.
On top of the wall is a walkway with benches for people to sit and enjoy
the view of the street through the branches of trees. Standing in the
roadway is architect Anthony Signorelli, who is drafting plans to move
the historic fieldstone Valentine-Varian House from across the
street to this spot.

AT BAINBRIDGE AVENUE AND VAN CORTLANDT AVENUE EAST,
the historic Valentine-Varian House built in 1758 is being moved across
Bainbridge Avenue from its original location on June 30, 1965.
The stone house, trussed with steel wire and placed on wheels, is being
dragged by cables pulled by trucks to the right across a temporary lumber
platform placed between curbs in the roadway. Traffic along Bainbridge
Avenue is halted by the police as local Norwood residents watch.
Reservoir Oval East and West, which had been separated from
Bainbridge Avenue by a pedestrian traffic island, has been reconstructed,
and a foundation has been dug upon which the house will be placed.
The house is slated to be used as a Museum of Bronx History
by The Bronx County Historical Society.

The Bronx County Historical Society
Research Library

THE CONSERVATORY IN THE NEW YORK BOTANICAL GARDEN
in the mid-1960s attracts visitors from around the world.
Its exotic tropical and desert plants are protected in its glasshouse
environment. Here, two visitors approach the main entrance,
a circular area topped by a cupola bearing several species
of palm trees.

The Bronx County Historical Society Research Library

167TH STREET JUST EAST OF THE GRAND CONCOURSE in 1938 stands the
Kent Theater. It specializes in double feature films that had already been shown
in other theaters. Here, it is the last night for viewing Olivia DeHavilland and
George Brent in "Gold is Where You Find It" and Annabella and William Powell in
"The Baroness and the Butler." In front of the marquee, a theater employee stands
atop the ladder replacing the old letters with new ones that will advertise the
incoming feature films. Next door, a candy and soda shop remains open to take
advantage of the leaving patrons, its wares advertised through the night by
a neon sign.

The Bronx County Historical Society
Research Library
—Ben Orange, photographer

Neighborhood
Life

*The Bronx County Historical Society
Research Library*

BAINBRIDGE AVENUE NORTH OF 194TH STREET in 1949 still has so little traffic that a neighborhood child can stand in the street without fear of oncoming traffic. Neighbor's cars, however, are beginning to fill in the parking spaces along the curbs. While there are such local shops as a delicatessen and a liquor store to the left and apartment houses in the distance, the street is dominated by handsome single-family homes along the tree-lined street.

MOUNT CARMEL ROMAN CATHOLIC CHURCH ON 187TH STREET BETWEEN BELMONT AND HUGHES AVENUES is the parish church for many residents of the predominantly Italian-American neighborhood of Belmont. Here, Monsignor Pernicone presides over one of the many weddings in the 1950s.

AT COLGATE AND WESTCHESTER AVENUES in the Soundview
neighborhood stands the Imperial Gardens catering hall.
Here, in November, 1946, Reverend Abraham Salkowitz
presides at a wedding ceremony.

A BAR MITZVAH, the Jewish ceremony that
marks the beginning of a thirteen year old boy's
entrance to adult religious life, is a major event
often marked by a family party and a formal
photograph. Here, in the Tremont Photo Studio
at 749 Tremont Avenue near Clinton Avenue
in the mid 1930s, a Bar Mitzvah Boy poses with
a prayerbook in his hand, a yarmulka on his head,
and a prayer shawl around his shoulders.

ST. ANN'S EPISCOPAL CHURCH ON ST. ANN'S AVENUE NEAR 140TH STREET is often the scene of patriotic ceremonies in the 1950s. Here, Lewis Morris, a Signer of the Declaration of Independence, and Gouverneur Morris, a Framer of the Constitution of the United States, are buried. Local veteran groups are represented at the ceremony, as well as local Boy and Sea Scouts in uniform. *The Bronx County Historical Society Research Library*

ASTOR AND SEYMOUR AVENUES is normally a quiet intersection of single family brick homes with plenty of trees and lawns. While there is light traffic in this eastern Bronx neighborhood just north of Pelham Parkway, an accident can always happen. Here in 1953, a truck owned by the Colonial Asphalt and Paving Company and weighing over 62,000 pounds slammed into the side of a Cadillac passenger car, causing rather serious damage.

The Bronx County Historical Society Research Library

SOUNDVIEW AVENUE AT THE JUNCTION OF WHITE PLAINS ROAD AND O'BRIEN AVENUE about 1958 illustrates the sparseness of the population and the wide open spaces near the eastern end of the Clason Point neighborhood. The tallest building is a slender five-story brick apartment house to the left. The others are two-story structures with the living quarters above street-level shops. Empty lots abound, and grass even grows in the cracks of the traffic island in the center, which also serves as a stop for the Soundview Avenue bus. Some of the houses are still heated by coal, as shown by the empty coal truck that is returning to its headquarters after making a delivery.

The Bronx County Historical Society Research Library–Seifert Collection

HAVEMEYER AVENUE AT THE INTERSECTION OF POWELL AVENUE in Unionport has a neat mixture of small apartment buildings and single family homes about 1947. The backyards are filled with clotheslines where wet wash is hung out to dry. The waters of Westchester Creek in the center right separate the neighborhood from Throggs Neck. Just below the horizon to the left, the elevated structure that carries the Lexington Avenue local subway trains can be seen. Punctuating the skyline in the center is the spire of St. Peter's Episcopal Church on Westchester Avenue just south of Westchester Square. *The Bronx County Historical Society Research Library*

GUN HILL ROAD SEEN FROM THE CORNER OF ROCHAMBEAU AVENUE looking west toward Jerome Avenue in 1952 is a street filled with traffic. While pedestrians stroll along the sidewalk shopping at the stores, trucks are forced to double park in order to deliver their goods because local residents have parked their late-model automobiles along the curb. A passing Lexington Avenue express train rumbles along the elevated structure above Jerome Avenue to the right. The apartment houses in the center rise above DeKalb Avenue, while other apartment structures can be seen beyond the elevated line along Knox Place. On the left are part of the grounds of Montefiore Hospital. *The Bronx County Historical Society Research Library*

DECATUR AVENUE LOOKING NORTH FROM 204TH STREET, soon after the record snowfall of December 26, 1947, shows a frosty winter scene. Although the superintendent of the apartment house to the left has dutifully cleared the sidewalk, the owners of the townhouses beyond have not yet done so, and the snow is still piled on the sidewalk. The cars parked at the curb have been completely buried under the snow, forming a continuous barrier for any pedestrian wishing to cross the street.

143RD STREET BETWEEN MORRIS AND THIRD AVENUES was just resurfaced with asphalt in 1952. One of the neighborhood boys is taking advantage of the situation by trying out his roller skates in the gutter. Cars flank the curb on both sides of the street. Aside from the Lester Patterson Houses, which flank the street, the neighborhood consists of walk-up apartment houses with shops at the sidewalk level.

THE BRONX RIVER JUST NORTH OF GUN HILL ROAD is in the process of receiving a new sewer in January, 1950. The bridge over the water in the center carries the Bronx River Parkway. Across the river, the rear of the DeSoto Sales and Service Center, the garage, and the moving and storage warehouse have their entrances on Webster Avenue. The apartment houses forming the skyline to the left are on Decatur Avenue south of 211th Street. The hill on the horizon and to the right is part of Woodlawn Cemetery.

*The Bronx County Historical Society
Research Library*

THIRD AVENUE AT 175TH STREET in 1956 is dominated by the Third Avenue El, which casts its shadow along the roadway. Parked cars hug the curbside. To the right is an apartment house and a line of shops at street level. To the left is a corner of Crotona Park. The destruction of the buildings near it is the first step in the construction of the Cross-Bronx Expressway through this part of the Tremont neighborhood. *The Bronx County Historical Society Research Library–Schleissman Collection*

CALDWELL AVENUE NORTH OF 149TH STREET in March, 1954, is the site of commercial and industrial structures built on top of a high rock outcropping overlooking the street to the left. Residents live in the apartment house overlooking the scene to the left, and in the attached townhouses arrayed along Trinity Avenue, seen above the roof of the building to the center left. On the horizon are the many apartment houses of the Morrisania neighborhood. *The Bronx County Historical Society Research Library*

ON THE WEST SIDE OF MORRIS AVENUE BETWEEN 154TH AND
156TH STREETS, houses are undergoing rehabilitation by Lindsey
Associates in the mid-1960s. At the street level is a storefront church,
the Universal Apostolic Church, with its signs in Spanish to appeal
to the surrounding Hispanic inhabitants. On the side of the building
to the left, an old, faded sign on the wall advertises Fletcher's Castoria.
It is partially obscured by a smaller, newer billboard sign for Hiram
Walker's Imperial whiskey, with its words in Spanish. On either side
of the American gas station to the right rises the new buildings of
the Concourse Village cooperative apartments.

AT WEST 230TH STREET NEAR TIBBETT AVENUE in 1964 stands an
Esso Station and its owner, Jimmy Packes. To the center right is Darby's
Wedge Inn, and, across Tibbett Avenue, is a Texaco Service Station.
The apartment houses face Johnson Avenue, and the Spuyten Duyvil
neighborhood rises on the hill behind them.

BOSTON ROAD AT VYSE AVENUE in June, 1956 is dominated by the elevated structure of the White Plains Road line of the Lexington Avenue subway. While a rock outcropping to the right shows that there is some empty space in this Tremont neighborhood area, Boston Road is dominated by commercial and industrial structures.

*The Bronx County Historical Society
Research Library
—Schleissman Collection*

BEDFORD PARK BOULEVARD BETWEEN DECATUR AND WEBSTER AVENUES in 1951 is the scene of street repair as a truck tilts its load backward to pour new asphalt onto the roadway, which is then smoothed by the steamroller located just behind the truck.
Some local residents watch the operation from the sidewalk.
One of the attached houses still has its windows shaded from the heat of the sun by awnings.

CROTONA AVENUE AT THE INTERSECTION OF 175TH STREET in 1956 is a street with light traffic, but whose curbs are filled with parked cars. The street is flanked by two-to five-story apartment houses. The lone tree in sight partially obscures a neighborhood delicatessen.

The Bronx County Historical Society Research Library

WASHINGTON AVENUE NEAR 170TH STREET is the site of an old Victorian house in February, 1956. Despite the fact that it is raised from the street and reached by a flight of stairs, the house boasts a tree growing from a front yard held in place by a stone retaining wall. A sign painted on that wall advertises radio repairs. The space at the right has been converted into a store occupied by a grocery selling Coca Cola, Seven Up, Salada Tea, Pabst Blue Ribbon Beer, and Camel cigarettes. The entire scene is slated for change, since the man in the roadway of Washington Avenue holding a sign stating "P186" is assisting a surveyor for the New York City Housing Authority. The Authority is planning to level the block to erect the Gouverneur Morris Houses on the site.

The Bronx County Historical Society Research Library

AT FERRY POINT IN THE VICINITY OF EMERSON AND MILES AVENUES in 1948 stands the old piers jutting out into Morris Cove where Baxter Creek meets the East River. On the horizon, the roadway of the Bronx-Whitestone Bridge meets the Queens shoreline.

The Bronx County Historical Society
Research Library

HAVILAND AVENUE LOOKING TOWARD HAVEMEYER AVENUE
in Unionport in an afternoon about 1947 shows almost an idyllic
scene as young pupils walk home from school along the deserted
roadway. Single-family frame homes with small manicured front
yards flank either side of the roadway, as four-story walk-up apartment
buildings dominate the corner of Havemeyer Avenue. Only three
cars are parked along the curb, and electricity is fed to the area by
way of wires strung from poles along the sidewalk.

The Bronx County Historical Society
Research Library

INDEX

179

LLOYD ULTAN is a professor of history at the Edward Williams College of Fairleigh Dickinson University in Hackensack, New Jersey. He served as president of The Bronx County Historical Society from 1971 to 1976, and is the author of articles and books on Bronx and American history, including the highly acclaimed *The Beautiful Bronx, 1920-1950*. He has also written, *Presidents of the United States* and *Legacy of the Revolution: The Story of the Valentine-Varian House* and is founding editor of *The Bronx County Historical Society Journal*.

GARY HERMALYN is the executive director of The Bronx County Historical Society, and president of the History of New York City Project, Inc. Author, editor, lecturer, and tour leader, he received his doctorate from Columbia University. He is the author of *Morris High School and the Creation of the New York City Public High School System*, co-author of *The Bronx in The Innocent Years, 1890-1925*, editor of the *Bicentennial of the United States Constitution* book series and *The Bronx County Historical Society Journal*, and associate editor of the *Encyclopedia of New York City*.

THE BRONX COUNTY HISTORICAL SOCIETY

THE BRONX COUNTY HISTORICAL SOCIETY was founded in 1955 for the purpose of promoting knowledge, research, and interest in The Bronx. The Society administers The Museum of Bronx History, Edgar Allan Poe Cottage, a research library, and The Bronx County Archives; publishes books, journals, and newsletters; conducts historical tours, lectures, courses, school programs, and commemorations; designs exhibitions; sponsors various expeditions; and produces cable TV programs and the "Out of the Past" radio show. The society is active in furthering the arts, in preserving the natural resources of The Bronx, and in creating the sense of pride in The Bronx community.

PUBLICATIONS OF
THE BRONX COUNTY HISTORICAL SOCIETY